ODYSSEY IN Love

ODYSSEY IN 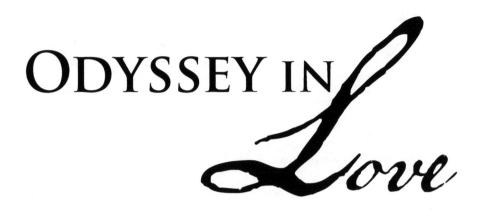Love

An Adventure in the Way, the Truth, and the Life

ROBERT A. YOUNG

iUniverse, Inc.
Bloomington

Odyssey in Love
An Adventure in the Way, the Truth, and the Life

iUniverse books may be ordered through booksellers or by contacting:

iUniverse
1663 Liberty Drive
Bloomington, IN 47403
www.iuniverse.com
1-800-Authors (1-800-288-4677)

ISBN: 978-1-4759-7862-9 (sc)
ISBN: 978-1-4759-7863-6 (ebk)

Library of Congress Control Number: 2013904767

Printed in the United States of America

iUniverse rev. date: 03/13/2013

Dedication:

This book is dedicated to my wife, *Mary Catherine Young*.

During one of my first encounters with Mary, she shared with me her conviction:

the power of a good woman is unlimited!

Wow! I was impressed then. And now, after 47 years of marriage, I am even *more* impressed as I begin to comprehend the magnitude of her statement.

The most noble act of a woman is to cooperate with God and her spouse and to create life . . . to create an eternal soul! That's right! A woman has the ability to create a unique, one-of-a-kind, spiritually perfect soul that lives for eternity. What a magnificent opportunity. What a profound responsibility.

Once a woman gives her *fiat*, her "*yes*", the human soul is created and incarnated. The woman then nurtures this "be-ing" both before and after physical birth. She invests her entire life helping to prepare this unique person, her child, for Eternity . . . for Heaven. This is the adventure of our existence!

I have participated in this adventure with my wife. But, lest you fail to understand, Mary is the *rock* of our family. Her children will attest to that! Her faith, her virtue, and her love have served to create and solidify our domestic church . . . our family . . . the Bob and Mary Young family. I thank our Providential God for giving me my spouse—my partner—for this adventure. She is the greatest blessing in my life.

I say to you Mary, my love, my good woman, this book is not the Taj Mahal. But the words herein will last longer than that most beautiful earthly memorial! For I say with conviction that the *words* in this book, which I call our "Odyssey in Love", will remain forever a testament to our "unlimited" eternal life!

With my eternal love, your husband, Bob Young

Preface:

I started writing this book in December of 1975. At the time, I didn't know I was writing a book. I was merely responding to a request from my wife, Mary, to help her. We were married in 1966. Every year thereafter she wrote personalized Christmas letters to all our friends. By late 1975, nine years later, we had five children and had just finished an exhausting move from Oregon to California. As an act of desperation she asked me to write a Christmas "form letter" to send out. My first reaction: "Are you kidding?" I **hate** those kinds of letters. I never read them. They are merely a litany of a family's accomplishments of the year. Boring, boring, boring . . . and yes, *really* boring.

Then I started to write our letter and was inspired by a Christmas letter I had received from one of my college roommates. His wife was the author of their letter. It was a litany of everything that had gone *wrong* that year. I found it to be hilarious.

Based on that inspiration, I wrote my first Christmas letter about our "*Odyssey*", that is, our "*journey*", from Portland, Oregon to Danville, California. My focus in the letter was to communicate our litany of experiences that year, *including our mishaps*, applying an attitude of Divine optimism.

We mailed out the letter, which I didn't think too much about. Then we had a married couple, Ron and Jan Miller, over for a visit one evening shortly thereafter. Mary suggested that we share the letter with them. We did. Jan read the letter aloud. She laughed so hard tears were flowing and she nearly fell off her chair. God bless you Jan, you pure soul, for your tacit encouragement! Jan left us for her heavenly reward several years ago. But if it weren't for her sincere and loving reaction to my boring form letter, I may never have written another. Jan, may your spirit be with us as this *Odyssey in Love*, this *Journey in God*, is shared with my progeny and to others who are searching for Home.

Thus, this book is a collection of the annual, boring, Young family Christmas letters, from 1975 through 2012. Also included in this book is the annual family Christmas picture that accompanied the letter. In addition, a very limited number of random pictures from that specific year are included if they relate to the story.

To set the stage for the first letter, there is a background chapter which journals *very briefly* some facts relative to the years 1966 through 1974, such as the location of our homes and the births of our children.

Due to the limitation of modern technology and my budget for this book, the pictures herein are not printed in color. To view them in color, go to my website at www.calltobefree.com. You will also find other useful information at this electronic home.

Morally speaking, the world is suffering through a time of darkness. Through faith and revelation, we know this will end. My hope is that, by reading this book, *you* will enhance your ability to see the Light that emanates from the Father; that *you too* will have an *adventure in the Son*, who is the Way, the Truth, and the Life!

Peace!

Bob Young

Background: 1966 to 1974

Our adventure began officially on June 15, 1966 in Saint Mary's Catholic Church, Richardton, North Dakota when we received the Sacrament of Matrimony.

After consummating our marriage contract we left North Dakota and headed for Helena, Montana, where Bob had a summer job with the US Forest Service and Mary had classes she needed to complete for her Bachelors degree. We drove our 1965 green Volkswagen "bug", loaded with *all* our earthly belongs, on our honeymoon through Yellowstone National Park along the way.

That fall we moved to Willow Creek, Montana, a town about 40 miles from Bozeman. I commuted to college at Montana State University in Bozeman to work on my Master's Degree in Math. Mary started teaching first grade in Willow Creek.

Early in 1967 Mary discovered that she was "with child." She resigned from her teaching position and we moved into an apartment in Bozeman.

Christie Lea Young was born in Bozeman on April 30, 1967. She was beautiful, of course!

I graduated with my Master's degree in Math and joined IBM in June of 1967. We moved to Great Falls, Montana where I was a "Systems Engineer", working with IBM customers to help them install and use their computers. Mary worked part-time as a kindergarten teacher.

Mary sent out personalized Christmas cards in December, along with our *first* Christmas picture!

In 1968 we bought our first house. It was beautiful! We paid $15,500 for the house complete with furniture. The prior owner was returning to college to get an advanced degree. The house was located at 820 53rd Street South. It had 850 square feet of space, which included two small bedrooms and one bathroom. It did have a full unfinished basement and a large fenced back yard.

Angela Therese Young was born on January 29, 1970. We were shocked when she arrived with blond hair!

We had some excitement immediately after Angela's birth. I was planning to leave Christie at a neighbor's house while I went to visit Mary and Angela in the hospital. As I crossed the street holding Christie, I slipped on some ice and fell. It turns out I broke my ankle and they had to take me to the hospital. Needless to say, Mary was somewhat surprised when I called her and said I couldn't come to her room since I was in bed on the floor below.

Meanwhile, Mary's mom, Eleanor, traveled from North Dakota to help. A couple of days after the falling accident, she noticed Christie moving gingerly. It turns out she had a broken collarbone!

Our second annual Christmas picture was taken in December of that year and shows the two sisters.

Nichole Noreen Young was born on June 9, 1971. Her arrival experience left Mary and me breathless! Since we had delivered two babies already, we felt we were very experienced with the entire process. So when Mary said she was having some initial labor pains, I expected that in a few days our new baby would arrive. I promptly went golfing with a friend. Remember, these were the days before the invention of cell phones. My friend and I finished nine holes and decided to stop since the queue for the second nine was too long. Upon arriving home, Mary said, "I think we better go to the hospital."

Upon arriving at the hospital, they took Mary away and I settled in to watch some TV. A few minutes later, they brought me into the labor room area and showed me my new daughter! Wow! I can still remember her large alert eyes staring at me as if I were some strange irresponsible creature from outer space. You should know that, many years later, she still looks at me the same way.

Our Christmas picture for 1971 is included below.

In the spring of 1972 I attended the IBM Systems Research Institute in New York City for three months. That summer I was promoted to Advisory Systems Engineer in Portland, Oregon. Mary and I moved with our three girls, Christie, Angela, and Nichole, into a very nice home in Beaverton. Our Christmas picture of 1972 is included below.

5 yr. 1 mo.   2 yr. 10 mo.   17 mo. 2 wk.

Our new home was located at 15125 NW Oakmont Loop in Beaverton. It was a ranch style home with four bedrooms and two bathrooms. The location was great. Our back yard abutted a large common green area and pool complex.

Here is a second picture of the house in Beaverton from another angle. Note the large, green, 1971 Buick Estate station wagon that is gracing the driveway. You will hear more about her later as she became a valued member of the Young family.

On May 30, 1973 Heidi Marie Young was born in Beaverton. She didn't have much hair, but what she did have was *red*! What was going on?

Our Christmas picture for 1973 is shown below. At this time, Mary is continuing to send out personalized Christmas card and letters, but is beginning to fall behind in the process.

On December 5, 1974 Robert Evan Young was born. By this time I was sure that I had some physical anomaly and that all my children were going to be girls. Not so! We had our first boy.

The reason this child was named "Robert", is that Mary and I had decided when we were married that we were not going to name our *first* boy "Robert" and our *first* girl "Mary." We agreed that the fifth child would be named Robert or Mary, depending upon the gender of course, and that the next child of the opposite gender would be named accordingly.

Our Christmas picture for 1974 is below. Since the face of Robert was difficult to see in the group picture, I cut out his face from another picture and glued it in the lower right hand corner. This is before the capability to do this existed with electronic photos and sophisticated software.

December 1975

Dear Friends,

Mary asked me to write a few words in the Christmas letter this year so please forgive the typing—I don't know how to write!

It has been an exciting year for the YOUNG'S! I accepted a promotion to a new job in San Francisco on Friday, June 13th. The new job is very challenging since in my area of responsibility we are doing worse than anywhere else in the United States. The fellow that had the job before me became frustrated and quit after two years. I am convinced that with dedication and hard work I will be able to maintain our record.

Our exodus from Portland was delayed somewhat when the sale of our house was held up after a water leak developed under the driveway. We were able to get this fixed for a couple of hundred dollars less than we expected. Then on closing day the fellow that was buying the house indicated he wanted out of the deal since he expected to get a job offer in another city. Fortunately for us his job offer fell through and he bought our house after all.

I'm certain that getting a man to the moon is no more complicated than moving a family of seven. Each pit stop was identified in advance as we drove from Portland to San Francisco in two days, limping from rest room to rest room. The kids were good considering the 100 degree heat.

Upon arriving in California we stayed in a motel for three weeks until our house deal closed. We ate in cafes frequently at first. Then Robert, my son, decided that mealtime was a convenient time to have a bowel movement. In one case we had to carry the high chair with him in it into the restroom for Mary to clean. After a few incidents we were able to reduce our meal expenses by cooking in the motel kitchenette.

We moved into our new home in time to celebrate my birthday. On the way to the store to get mousetraps Mary and Heidi were in an accident with the 1965 Green Volkswagen. They were both really shook up and Mary had to have several stitches in her cheek. We are all so grateful that no one was seriously hurt. Even Mary's scar is not visible when she is seated.

My faithful car did not fare so well, however. With 107,000 miles on her sturdy engine she is now traveling that great highway in the sky. One can only conjecture about the additional contributions she may have made had her life not been so violently snuffed out.

It was shortly after the car accident that Christie broke her arm. Luckily it was her right arm since she is left-handed. She broke two bones in the same arm last year.

We are really thankful the doctor did such a good job sewing up Angela's chin after she fell and hit it. The doc only needed seven stitches. He says her scar may not be too bad.

Nichole's scar on her chin is healing well. It is more under her chin and not very noticeable. She had to have eight stitches after hitting the side of the swimming pool in Portland earlier this summer.

It only took about two weeks to repair the Buick after my accident. The other two cars weren't so lucky. The first one I hit was totaled and the second one had about

$1,500 damage—same as mine. I don't think any of the four people that were injured are seriously hurt although a couple of them were shaken up pretty badly. I have to go to court soon as they want to give me a citation. I'm pleased that my insurance company has been so responsive.

Mary hasn't had to get her hands in any dishwater lately. The doctor keeps putting acid on her warts to remove them and I guess water washes away the acid. This is good because it gives Christie and Angela a chance to do some housework.

I have really been able to keep up on the news since we've moved. The two and one-half hours I spend commuting every day allows me time to read both the morning and evening papers. Although I used to get sick when I read while riding in a moving vehicle, that doesn't seem to be a problem anymore. Perhaps it's because now I usually read while in a standing position.

The fellow that is repairing our furniture is doing a pretty good job. Almost everything was damaged during the move. The most damage was done to the beautiful new bedroom set we bought the day before we left Portland.

Our new house has some really neat features: air conditioning, large yard, and built in lawn sprinklers with automatic timers. Fortunately our electric bill has not been that high because we disconnected the air conditioning after we all caught colds. At first we had a lot of lawn and shrubbery clippings that we had to pay to get removed. Then the lawn caught a fungus disease from too much water and died so now we don't water it and have a lot fewer clippings to worry about. It seems as if problems just take care of themselves.

Of course the cost of living in California is much higher than Oregon. The taxes on our new home are about the same as my entire house payment, including taxes, in Portland. We are really lucky, though. With all the interest and property taxes I'm paying plus the losses I've had in the stock market, I will be able to pay my income tax with green stamps this year.

Mary and I are really excited about the prospect of someone drilling for oil on some mineral acres we own in North Dakota. A company has leased these mineral rights and is paying us 1/4 of 5/160 of $160 per year ($1.25) on a five year lease for the right to drill on our land. If they find oil on the land, we will get 1/4 of 5/160 of 1/8 of what they find. I think the $12 it cost me to have all the legal papers notarized could be offset by the potential gain if we strike oil. With a little luck I'll get at least one oil change for my lawnmower.

Mary and I still consider our marriage a ball! This feeling is particularly heightened on Saturday and Sunday afternoons during our scheduled nap time when we have a chance to contemplate the fun of married life.

Merry Christmas! May Peace and Happiness be yours in 1976.

Bob, Mary, and family

Christmas Picture 1975

Below is a picture of our new home at 826 Glen Road, Danville, California. It had five bedrooms, two and a half bathrooms, and a three car garage!

Here is another view of our California home. The home, including the garage, was 100 feet long! With the used brick as a façade all along the front, it was very impressive looking. Mary and I couldn't believe that we were living in such a ritzy place.

December 1976

Dear Friends,

Another year has passed and Mary has again asked me to write a few words in the Christmas letter.

This year was somewhat uneventful for the YOUNG'S! After moving to Danville last year, life has settled into a pretty relaxing routine.

We went to Los Angeles and Disneyland this year for our vacation. We stayed with Toni and Dave, Mary's sister and her family, for a week. During our stay we visited Disneyland twice, once with our five kids and Toni with her four kids, and once with our four oldest kids. We saw and rode *everything*! God bless you Walt Disney! We decided that Toni deserved a break for putting up with 7 extra people for a week so Mary and I took the nine kids to the San Diego zoo and a quick trip into Mexico. We also went swimming with the kids one day. The kids all agreed: they really had a fun, relaxing vacation this year.

One person that was injured in my car accident last year is suing me for $50,000. My insurance company has been reluctant to pay for his medical bills. They can't understand how a whiplash could cause him to need an operation to remove cysts on his bladder.

Our chandelier in the kitchen went on the blink this summer. After eating in the dark for several months I decided to call an electrician. After waiting for six more weeks I decided to fix it myself so I took it all apart twice and rechecked all the wiring and the connections. Then Mary suggested that we check the bulbs and we discovered that four of the five bulbs were burned out. Mary feels she is pretty lucky to have a husband that can fix things around the house. We also wallpapered our bedroom and the utility room. We ran out of paper twice in the bedroom and once in the utility room.

Mary and I are teaching a method of natural birth control in a family planning class. We really enjoy it. We became involved in this shortly before she became pregnant. She is due in May of next year. We are looking forward to number "6".

The kids have really taken an interest in reading and other activities lately. I noticed the change shortly after Robert tipped over the color TV and shattered the picture tube.

Fortunately this year my house taxes went up 30% again. By keeping pace with my increases in income, the additional deduction will allow me to keep my income tax down again this year.

In October I was promoted to systems engineering manager with IBM in Oakland. The commute is much better now: 20 miles and 30 minutes. This is about half of what it was traveling to downtown San Francisco. I cannot use public transportation to get to my new job however, so Mary and I decided to replace the Volkswagen she destroyed last year with a new car. It's always difficult to handle additional payments, but Mary is very frugal and we have found, for example, that a significant amount of money can be saved by having the kids pass on their shoes from one to another as they grow older. We keep all their used shoes in a big box and anytime someone needs a different pair, there's just no problem finding one. I really enjoy driving my Mercedes to work—it handles so nice. It makes so much noise when it starts (diesel) the kids call it "Dad's tractor."

I traveled to Connecticut for a one week class in November. What I thought was side effects from my swine flu shot turned out to be a bleeding ulcer. By the time I realized something was wrong and went to the hospital, I had lost about half my blood. After pumping eleven pints of blood into me and starving me to stop the bleeding, I recovered quite rapidly. I'm sure everyone's prayers helped. In fact, several people continued praying even after I healed so now I have the body of an 18-year-old. IBM flew Mary out to be with me in the hospital and flew her mom from North Dakota to California to babysit our kids. While in the hospital I panicked when I realized our plans for a large family was jeopardized. They had been giving me "sterile water" for four days. Fortunately for me the electricity went out briefly while I was in the hospital which allowed me to have a pleasant bowel movement. The refrigerator in which the bed pans were kept was inoperative for some time. The hospital where I stayed was unusual in that a high percentage of nurses there had apparently failed their course in "rectal thermometer insertion." I wonder if they would try to thread a needle with their eyes closed. I became very jumpy after several misses. I watched the janitor nearly have a heart attack. One afternoon when Mary was visiting, she decided to take a little nap on the floor. I guess finding a body laying on the floor in a hospital would be a little disconcerting.

We went to a Christmas party last night. Mary had bought a new dress and we were really excited. We ended up getting there about 45 minutes late because we had a little trouble finding the home of a new babysitter. It turns out we were eight days early. Needless to say the hosts were a little surprised to see us.

I will not guarantee a Christmas picture of the kids next year. I have done a mathematical analysis of the probability involved in getting six kids to sit still and smile at the same time. This year it took 24 pictures to produce one rather mediocre pose. It turns out that the probability of getting a good picture decreases exponentially with the inverse of the square of the ages of the children under the age of seven. Thus next year we will have to start taking pictures in August to statistically produce a good picture by December. By the time we have 10 kids, I hope to convince Mary to take separate pictures of the kids and have them photo reduced onto one picture or I'll end up being a full time photographer.

Mary and I are still on a honeymoon. It seems as if we "know" (as in the Biblical sense) each other more all the time. Reminds me of the man who said to his doctor, "Doc, I think my libido is waning." The doctor asked, "How old are you and your wife?" The man said, "I'm 85 and she's 83." The doctor continued, "When did you notice this?" The man said, "Well, first last night and then again this morning."

Merry Christmas! May Peace and Happiness be yours in 1977.

Bob, Mary, and Family

Christmas Picture 1976.

This is me with my new 1976 yellow Mercedes. I would never have thought to buy such a fine car, except my lovely wife, Mary, wanted me to be "safe" and felt that this car was designed to accomplish that.

December 1977

Dear Friends,

Mary insisted I write a short note again this Christmas despite that fact that it has been a very routine year for the YOUNG'S!

"If it's yellow, let it mellow. If it's brown, flush it down." This is our motto now that we are on water rationing due to the drought. With a water quota equal to 20% of last year's usage, the 7 gallons of water needed to flush a toilet becomes significant. Putting bricks in the toilet tank reduces each flush to about 3 gallons. Last summer when the high coffee prices and water shortage hit at the same time, the recommendation was to put bricks in your coffee.

Mary (8 months pregnant) and I took the kids on a weekend trip to Lake Tahoe in April and went sliding down the mountain on inner tubes. We really enjoyed the trip. However, the logistics of taking the kids out to eat, dressing each of them with two pair of mittens, snow-boots, snow-pants, sweater, coat and scarf, then taking them potty, carrying Robert and pushing Mary up the hill, driving 150 miles home listening to several loud versions of "hundred bottles of beer on the wall", left me near the verge of a mental collapse. Upon discerning my near recovery, Mary suggested we drive the family to North Dakota for a vacation next year. Undaunted by past experience and unable to resist the challenge, I have begun preparing mentally for what may be my most formidable undertaking to date!

Ryan Paul was born May 4th. Our "baby" is now 22 pounds at 7 months. As a result of constantly carrying him around, Mary's biceps have developed to the point that I'm trying to convince her to enter the National Arm Wrestling championships. The kids have stopped eating candy since Ryan was born. When Mary was eating lots of candy before Ryan came, I told them that candy makes your teeth fall out. When Ryan was born with no teeth, they believed me.

As anticipated, the taking of our Christmas picture this year was no small task. We took the kids to one of those "pixie" photographers. The girl was a little flustered until she realized that only 6 of the 8 kids belonged to us. We were babysitting for a friend. None of those pictures turned out, so I finally took several myself. Imagine trying to get 12 eyes all looking the same direction simultaneously.

I'm so proud of my wife for always being so practical. For example, this year for my birthday she gave me two toilet seats. It's a gift the whole family can use. Another time I returned our two year old mattress to Sears because it sagged too much. After getting the new one and noticing the same problem, Mary showed me how to fix it by putting *straight* boards under the bed.

I have had no more stomach problems since last year. We are certainly blessed to have quality medical care in this great nation. The other night Mary and I were reflecting on how good a year it was. Our family is fine. Inflation is down. Employment is up. Even the Middle East situation has been changed by Egyptian (Muslim) Anwar

Sadat's peace trip to Israel. I commented to Mary that I thought the trip was very "Christian" of him.

Merry Christmas! May Peace and Happiness be yours in 1978.

Bob, Mary, and Family

Christmas Picture 1977.

Mary and I had a romantic overnight get-away in San Francisco. This picture was taken when we were out to dinner in early 1978.

December 1978

Dear Friends,

Just another short note from the YOUNG'S.

As I mentioned last Christmas, Mary had convinced me to drive to North Dakota for our vacation this year. Fortunately I was promoted by IBM shortly before we left so it was a one way trip to New York State where we now live.

Thanks to the many friends who let us stay overnight along the way, we had a delightful trip through California, Oregon, Washington, and Montana. My 1971 Buick Estate station wagon held up quite well. The fuel pump didn't go out until we were just outside Great falls, Montana. It happened right after the near head-on collision. Luckily I was driving since Mary had forgotten her contact lenses in California and couldn't drive. I was able to hit the ditch in time to miss the other car that was passing on a hill. The ignition system on the Buick didn't go out until two days later.

The kids were sick by the time we got to Billings, Montana. Herpes, ear infections, and tonsillitis were present in various combinations among the kids with Ryan, the baby, having all three.

It was at Williston, North Dakota where Jack, my brother-in-law, and I were almost shot on the golf course. I guess they shoot the gophers there and a ricocheting bullet narrowly missed us.

We arrived at Mary's folks about a week before the family reunion. I made breakfast one morning. It was the first time I had ever made 140 pancakes for one meal. There were 23 people staying in the house. It was sometimes hard to tell when one mealtime stopped and another started. I left alone for New York to go house-hunting, leaving the rest of the family with the grateful grandparents. By this time several of my father-in-law's cattle, originally destined to become "Big Mac's", had graced the dinner table and served to subdue several voracious appetites.

The Buick seemed to degenerate as I proceeded from North Dakota to New York via Minnesota, Iowa, Illinois, Indiana, Ohio, Pennsylvania, and New Jersey. Tortured by the heat and my relentless pace, her once strong body was now straining mentally and physically as her odometer rolled over the 82,000 mile mark. Following my arrival in New York, exploratory surgery was performed. After a serious analysis, the mechanic closed her back up and gave the following prognosis, "She has only a short time to live."

Shocked at first, I was unable to accept the chilling reality. Hoping to give her some solace in her final days, I had her carburetor cleaned, replaced her voltage regulator, and adjusted her fuel mixture. Despite occasional burps of black smoke, she has responded marvelously to the treatment. Knowing she may expire at any moment, she is approaching her final days with a vibrant courage and graceful dignity.

My house-hunting trip was successful. Having found a typical New England white, two-story colonial house, Mary flew out to join me and give her approval. She really liked the house, too. Then we went back to California where we completed the sale of our other house, said goodbye to all our friends, and got the mover with his truck on his way. From there we went to North Dakota to pick up the kids and then to New York with an overnight stay in Chicago. We stayed in a motel for two weeks awaiting the moving van. Luckily I didn't have to pay for the motel room door after using a hack saw to remove Ryan from the locked room.

My Mercedes is repaired now. There was $600 damage when the mover backed the car out of the truck over his metal dolly.

Cleaning the new house proved to be a formidable task. We started by fumigating it. Then we spent two days and six bottles of ammonia on the kitchen. Interestingly, the dirt was holding the cupboards together so we are now having a new kitchen put in. We did find something to clean the bathroom tile. The acid worked so well, however, we may have to replace the fixtures.

Mary was convinced there was an unusual odor coming from the basement. Luckily when an electrician was stringing some wire, the dead mouse was discovered. I should have known. Every time Mary is pregnant her sense of smell is heightened. The baby is due July 5th. Mary wanted to have it then so she wouldn't have to be pregnant during the hot summer.

To live in New York State, one has to accept the oppressive taxes and high utility bills. This will be the first year my property taxes will be more than my combined federal and state taxes. The famous Con Ed utility company provides us with electricity and gas. After I found out utility bills of $300 a month are common in the winter months, I have been busily replacing light bulbs. I didn't know until now that they even made 7.5 watt light bulbs. One night we thought there was a problem with the electricity. The night light kept blinking on and off. I read my new do-it-yourself book to no avail. Then we found out that Mary had replaced the old bulb with a blinking Christmas light.

Lately Ryan has a habit of putting both his index fingers up his nostrils. Mary was giving him heck for picking his nose until I pointed out that she should be pleased that he is ambidextrous.

The schools are excellent here. Before we moved here, we always used to kid Heidi and Nichole about their New York accent. We were surprised when they put them in speech therapy.

The fellow that is suing me is on his second set of lawyers. The first set has put a lien for their fees against any future judgment. He finally specified an amount he wanted: $70,000 more than my insurance will cover. Well, as they say, "Easy come, easy go." Perhaps he would settle for a nice 1971 Buick station wagon—just like new!!!!

Merry Christmas! May Peace and Happiness be yours in 1979.

Bob, Mary, Christie, Angela, Nichole, Heidi, Robert, and Ryan

This is our Christmas Picture for 1978. It was taken on Bedloe's Island, where the Statue of Liberty is located. Note the Manhattan skyline is in the background.

This is the home we bought at 5 Noyes Drive in Mount Kisco, New York. It had six bedrooms and 5.5 bathrooms and a beautiful one-acre lot. We were amazed that we the purchase price on this property was only slightly more than the money we got for our house in California.

Here is another view of the house in Mount Kisco.

Here is a view of the back of the house in Mount Kisco.

Here is a picture of the fountain in the back yard of our house in Mount Kisco.

December 1979

Dear Friends,

Mary asked me to drop you a short note again this year, despite the fact that it has been an uneventful year for the YOUNG'S.

This was the year our new kitchen and associated remodeling, scheduled for completion in December 1978, was finished by the contractor—on April Fool's Day. Actually the delay proved very beneficial since it gave Robert and Ryan an extended opportunity to watch the workers tear down walls, chip out the entryway tile, install plumbing, wiring, windows, doors, wallboards, etc. The boys enjoyed watching the dust fly, especially the fine white dust caused by sanding dried spackling paste. Also, eating in the living room and helping their pregnant mother wash dishes in the bathroom seemed to entertain them. Another benefit was to eliminate their TV viewing for 3 months since that room was closed off to keep the dust in the rest of the house.

Mary is big on volume buying lately. She had a little trouble the other day, however, when the store refused to give her a rain check for 100 pounds of hamburger on sale. She had to make a special trip to the store the next day after they refilled the meat counter. According to my calculations, volume buying does pay. She just bought two cases of toilet paper at 20% off. That amounts to a savings of approximately 5/100 of a cent per average wipe. You can't turn up your nose at that!

There seems to be a status symbol associated with imports. You know, everyone seems to have imported beer, cheese, cars, etc. We have joined the bandwagon. We imported two mousetraps from North Dakota.

Marianne Rachelle was born July 3rd. We wanted to do something special, so we requested a home baptism. We didn't get approval despite my phone call to Cardinal Cooke and my telegram to the Pope. Anyway the local priest did give her a real special Baptism during Mass on Sunday. In September we took her to the Mass conducted by Pope John Paul II at Yankee Stadium. She really seemed to enjoy it, especially when she was nursing.

Angela's hair has grown back already. A portion of her head was shaved so the large gash resulting from hitting her head on the diving board could be stitched up by the doctor. For some reason they didn't shave Robert's head before stitching up his cut.

Christie will need a new pair of left-handed scissors. Hers were ruined when the metal was fused together. Mary knew exactly when it happened because all the lights in the house dimmed when Ryan put the scissors against some live wires in a broken socket. Ryan has been real good about not doing that any more.

Some people claim that music relaxes them. With the three oldest kids taking piano lessons plus Christie taking flute and Angela clarinet, I *should* be very relaxed.

According to the news yesterday, the Disco craze is over. Mary and I will finish our 10th and last lesson next week.

The opportunity arose to test out my drainage system this year. One day while I was at work, it rained three inches in half an hour. I really laughed when Mary described how she ran up and down the outdoor basement stairs in her underpants, frantically hauling out water in buckets. During supper that evening it started to rain again and rained another three inches in half an hour. Well, at least when I carried the water out I kept my pants on!

According to the lawyer representing my insurance company and me, the lawsuit filed against me in 1975 may be nearly over. It looks as if the plaintiff will accept an amount $1,000 over the amount we offered him in 1976. The insurance company representing the third party in the accident will contribute the extra money. Apparently my lawyer pointed out to the judge during the settlement conference that it was futile for the plaintiff to get money from me in that my assets consisted of 7 children under the age of 12.

Following a valve job, my faithful, gallant 1971 Buick Estate station wagon has a new lease on life. However she does seem to be a little jumpy lately. A few scrapes and dents now mar her once graceful sleek body. Fortunately, the driver was not in the parked car at the time Mary hit it. Also, the garage wall can be patched.

My Mercedes has the jitters too. Neither the garage steps nor the retaining wall in the driveway were damaged badly when she hit them. The neighbor's tree is okay also. Luckily, the car was not rolling too fast. Mary had left the car on a hill and had failed to set the parking brake. The kids subsequently knocked it out of gear. They were able to jump out of the car as it rolled down the hill.

I decided I don't need to repair my TV after all, now that I have eyeglasses.

The entire family is healthy and happy. We all enjoy living in the New York area.

Merry Christmas! May Peace and Happiness be yours in 1980.

Bob, Mary, Christie (12), Angela (9), Nichole (8), Heidi (6),
Robert (5), Ryan (2), Marianne (6 mo.), . . . ?

Christmas Picture 1979.

March 1981

Dear Friends,

Merry Christmas from the YOUNG'S! Mary asked me to write a short note again. We decided to send Christmas cards in March this year since December is such a busy month.

I've noticed people talk about their health a lot as they get older. I guess Mary and I are no exception. Luckily she came through her operation successfully.

I guess everything just wears out as it gets older. I'll never forget the feeling I had as she lay there and a greenish fluid dripped from her tired body. Memories flooded my mind as I recalled the many special places we went together. As I lovingly caressed her sturdy frame, I was overcome with emotion as I faced the stark realization that the end was near. The third operation in less than a year has given us new hope however. The new radiator system seems to be just what she needed. With that, plus a "new" rebuilt alternator and a new master brake cylinder, my 1971 Buick Estate station wagon embarks upon the twilight of her years with dignity and grace.

I babysat for a week while Mary had her hernia operation. Things were tough until Mary told the kids that I was the Boss and they should listen to me.

Speaking of health, Mary and I are trying to lose weight like so many other people. We've tried several approaches. One was to take Mary out to dinner every two weeks to celebrate her losing a pound. At the end she weighed 65. I was really impressed with her progress until I discovered the switch on our new electronic scale was set to kilograms rather than pounds! . . . The other night we were eating popcorn and I mused that I had become rather "portly." Mary agreed. Later I found out she thought I had said "porky."

My medical condition has improved substantially since the World Series. As you know, George Brett, the famous third basemen for the Kansas City Royals, had a serious hemorrhoid issue also and needed to have surgery. In my case, I decided surgery was too drastic a solution. My treatment proceeded fairly routinely until I inadvertently left the Preparation H suppositories in the grocery bag with four loaves of bread—which I put in the deep freeze. The expression "chills up my spine" now has a special meaning for me. But I feel the same as George Brett who commented about his condition, "My problems are all behind me."

Well, like California, I don't have to spend much money on lawn fertilizer here either. The neighbor's dog had an operation to remove his tail, and they cut too deeply. Now his sphincter muscle doesn't work. It's a good deal for the dog also as it never gets constipated any more.

Mary and I went to a dance and won a prize for the best costume representing the 1950's. We didn't know there was a contest.

The other night I woke myself up by laughing so hard at something Mary had said in my dream. The *older* she gets, the *funnier* she gets.

Mary has now devised a way to make her shopping tax deductible. She is selling wall-hangings to retail stores. Everything was going well until one store owner wanted to buy something from her and she got all flustered because she didn't know how to take an order.

I have a new job with IBM. I am now manager of a small group that is trying to improve the way we fix **errors** in the IBM computer programs our customers are using. As I excitedly explained my new job at the dinner table, Angela said, "How depressing."

The kids are doing fine. Christie is a teenager, bashful and meek when she's not at home. Angela is the musician and clown. Nichole is the social butterfly. Heidi is the artist. Robert, . . . his first year in kindergarten, sets puzzles and challenges the "truths" stated by his father. Ryan spends his time eating, watching Sesame Street, and eating. When his grandmother offered him a dollar as she was leaving last fall, he wouldn't take it because he already had one. Marianne is 20 months old and has kept things lively this last year. The first time she came down the stairs head over heels, Mary cried—she didn't. She now makes it down that flight of stairs in exactly 4 seconds by sliding on her stomach like a seal. Mary potty trained her with M&M candies. She bribed her by giving her one every time she went. Marianne's dentist was impressed that such a small child could be potty trained.

One of our kid's friends was over the other night. It was obvious her parents believe in ecumenism. When asked what religion she was, she replied, "Half Jewish and half Christian."

Hope you have a happy and healthy year.

Bob, Mary, Christie (13), Angela (11), Nichole (9), Heidi (7),
Robert (6), Ryan (3), and Marianne (20 mo.)

Christmas picture March 1981.

Below is a picture of Bob and Mary in front of the family fountain taken in the summer of 1980.

June 1982

Dear Friends,

Merry Christmas from the YOUNG'S! Mary asked me to write a short note again to tell you of the years' activities. As you can see by the date of this letter, we are now on a *fiscal* year of July to July.

Defying all earlier predictions of her imminent demise, THE 1971 Buick Estate station wagon took us and our belongings to Chicago on the first leg of a 6,000 mile trek that Mary refers to as our "vacation." From Chicago we went to North and South Dakota and Eastern Montana with a truck-camper borrowed from my philanthropic, but nervous, brother-in-law. We graciously left the Buick for him to use. Outfitted with new seat covers and a new muffler, her façade of respectability was diminished only by a flat tire and a failing air conditioner.

We are thankful to all the beautiful people who gave us lodging and food along the way. We needed a motel room only one night. I'm sure Holiday Inn didn't have us in mind when they said kids could stay free with their parents. With nine people in one room, the "facilities" were somewhat overtaxed. The bathroom should have had a revolving door. We panicked the next morning—Marianne was missing! Later we found her sleeping *under* our bed, much to our relief.

The trip was a formidable physically as it was mentally. Two weeks before we left, I fell off a ladder onto my back. Luckily the cracked bone only caused pain when I was sitting, standing, lying down, or walking.

On December 6th Mary went to the hospital to have a large growth removed . . . we call him Russell James. He has *red* hair and a big smile.

All the kids are doing fine. Four of them are playing soccer, three are playing softball, one is playing baseball, three are taking piano lessons, three are in band, and two are in choir. With practices, games, concerts, recitals, and a couple of birthday parties sandwiched in between, I look forward to getting to the office every Monday morning to relax.

Last Sunday, while attending my third soccer game and leisurely dulling my senses with a cold beer, I was asked to be "linesman." I was told my job was to identify the team that kicked the ball out-of-bounds, and call out the shirt color of the opposing team. I had already accepted the assignment before I realized my color-blindness prevented me from detecting any difference between the red (maroon) shirts of one team and the blue shirts of the other. However, I was able to tell the color of their shorts: one team had red and the other white. Unfortunately, the team with the red shorts had the blue shirts, and the team with the red shirts had the white shorts. I'm sure you understand why I became *speechless* when the first out-of-bounds occurred. When I finally did call out a color, I was amazed at how upset everyone got. Luckily, the effects of the beer kept me from taking any of their remarks personally.

Marianne is doing well. She had the stitches taken out of her knee last week. Also, she doesn't have cancer. About a month after she ate Mary's contact lens, she developed a persistent runny nose and a terrible bad breath. After five weeks we took her to the doctor who found the problem. She had stuffed a large piece of newspaper up her nose and it was rotting. She will be three in July.

Ryan continues to amaze us with the piano. He teaches himself songs. After his party for his 5th birthday, he went to the piano and played "Happy Birthday."

Robert, at age 7, is an eating machine with hair. Heidi, Nichole, and Angela are all playing soccer on boy's teams this year. I must have checked the wrong box when I signed them up. They don't seem to mind. Christie and Angela discovered their teeth. I gave them a choice between a college education and the orthodontist; they chose the orthodontist. When I told them they could eat corn on the cob through venetian blinds, I didn't realize they would take me seriously.

At 101,000 miles the "green bomb" continues to amaze us. Will she make it another year? Will Mary and I keep our sanity for another year? Tune in next year for another installment.

Have a healthy and happy year!

Bob, Mary, Christie (15), Angela (12), Nichole (11), Heidi (9), Robert (7), Ryan (5), Marianne (2), and Russell (6 mo.)

Christmas picture sent out June of 1982.

Here is a picture of Bob and Mary in August of 1981.

Here is a picture of the Young family in Chicago en route to North Dakota in the summer of 1981. The famous green Buick Estate station wagon is behind us. Mary is pregnant with Russell. Note the large home-made white box on top of the station wagon which was used for storage. Mini-vans were not invented yet. The camper belonging to Orrin and Mary Jean Moen is in the background. We took that from Chicago to North Dakota and back.

This is a picture of Bob and Mary in March of 1982.

December 1983

Dear Friends,

Merry Christmas from the YOUNG'S! Mary asked me to write a short note again. We intended to send out Christmas cards in June again, like last year, but were delayed. Hope you don't mind.

I'm sure you are waiting to hear the news. Yes, *the* 1971 Buick wagon is still alive, having traveled over 107,000 miles. (I'm told this is the equivalent of a dog living 19 years.) Her creaking green body, with engine smoking and fluids dripping, responds with reckless abandon to Christies' 16-year-old touch, blissfully unaware of the many "close calls." Christie just started work part-time as a checker at the local supermarket. Last summer we rented out her and Angela as mother's helpers.

To celebrate our 17th anniversary, Mary and I splurged last March and flew to Cancun, Mexico *alone* for a week of fun. We thoroughly enjoyed ourselves. During the day we basked in the sun and baked our brains and buns. During the warm, tropical night we relaxed to the soothing rhythm of the surf massaging the broad, expansive, white sandy beach. My attack of "Montezuma's Revenge" and unsettled stomach only lasted one day—the day we took the 6 hour bus ride to visit the Mayan ruins. My Boy Scout training paid off. I brought along a roll of toilet paper and a plastic bag. Both were desperately needed that day.

We returned and were informed of a tragedy in the neighborhood. Our neighbor had been vacuuming her bird cage, and had forgotten to first remove the bird.

Last summer the entire family made a pilgrimage to North Dakota in our new 15 passenger Dodge Maxi-van, stopping only to refuel with Chicken McNuggets. Mary's sisters, Stephie and Lori, were married the same week. All the relatives came. The Hoff's 21 grandchildren had a great time, especially at the wedding dances. Apparently Stephie was very "tired" after her wedding. Still wearing her wedding gown, she was given a speeding ticket as she raced to the motel after the wedding dance.

Every time we went into McDonalds, Ryan, age 6, would grab a bunch of straws, which were all over the floor by the time the drinks came. Finally, in exasperation, I told him to never take straws the rest of my life. He took the news calmly and, with an odd look on his face, responded, "Okay, Dad. But when you die it will be my responsibility."

Ryan's first tooth fell out and he lost it. Luckily he was able to borrow one of Robert's old teeth so he could get money from the tooth fairy.

We bought the kids an Atari video game. Robert, age 9, talked me into playing with him. Later I heard him tell Mary, "For an old person, Dad plays really well."

I did turn "40" this year. In order to show everyone how "Young" I was, I joined Angela, Nichole, Robert, and Heidi in a 6 mile race. Angela came in first, with myself and Robert right behind. The three of us finished in under an hour with Nichole and Heidi finishing a few minutes later.

At age 13 going on 14, Angela is definitely a teenager. She has now recognized how "old fashioned" her parents are.

Nichole, age 12, received a very large sportsmanship trophy for her activities on the swim team last summer. Whenever she fights with the other kids at home now, we call her "Miss Sportsmanship."

Heidi, age 10, is our Girl Scout and Saturday morning babysitter. She and Nichole gave me some advice when we had our kitchen chairs re-covered. Since I am color-blind, and Mary wasn't home, they helped me pick out the colors. When we got the chairs back, I told Mary not to worry. No color blind person would notice the newly covered chairs didn't match the other kitchen colors.

The two youngest kids made the obligatory trip to the hospital emergency room this year: Marianne, age 4, to get the gum out of her nose; and Russell, age 2, to get his lip sewn up after his stroller accident. Heidi also went in for an asthma attack. I went for a heart attack . . . that turned out to be indigestion. Mary had to go to the hospital to have a cyst removed from her foot. While operating on her, the doctor asked how many children she had. Later, when Mary asked him to put a zipper in her foot, rather than stitches, he suggested she talk to her gynecologist. When she finally did get to the gynecologist, he informed us that number "9" will be joining us around the fourth of July next year.

We celebrated Russell's second birthday tonight. Mary left around eight to go to a party, telling me he is now potty trained so not to put a diaper on him. He's only pooped his pants once so far this evening.

Seems like Mary and I are so busy lately we don't have time to keep up this house like we did our other houses. Finally, Mary *insisted* I wash the walls. After washing for an hour, I ran into the kitchen and told her I found a sliding glass door I didn't know we had.

At age 4, Marianne gives indications of being a philosopher. Recently, Mary asked her, "Do you love *me* as much as I love *you*?" Marianne replied, "How much do *you* love *me*?"

I read the other day that death is nature's way of telling us to slow down.

Have a healthy and happy year!

Bob, Mary, Christie (16), Angela (13), Nichole (12), Heidi (10), Robert (9), Ryan (6), Marianne (4), Russell (2), and??? (-7mo.)

Christmas picture December of 1983.

Here is Mary in Cancun Mexico in March of 1983. What a cool body for a 37 year-old mother with eight kids!

Here is Mary all dressed to go out for the evening. She looks like a movie star!

Children of the Young family, here is a close-up photo of your mother at age 37 with a great tan after a few days in the sun.

Here is the Young family traveling to North Dakota in our new 1983 Dodge Maxi-van.

December 1984

Dear Friends,

Merry Christmas from the YOUNG'S! Mary asked me to drop you a note and update you on the happenings over the past year.

Well, I'm sure you are probably anxious to hear how the 1971 Buick station wagon is faring. She now has 113,000 miles on her stately body, her pride only slightly tarnished by the large dent in her fender (Christie tried to share one lane of traffic with another car). We were able to give her a muffler transplant following a lengthy search for a suitable donor. Also, her color seems to have improved after the technicians repaired her heater and leaking circulation system. Her foreign compatriot, the 1976 Yellow Mercedes at 110,000 miles, now threatens to exceed her in mileage.

Everyone wanted "Cabbage Patch" dolls this year. It was the craze. Mary was no exception. She wanted one. We call her Heather Anne. She was born on July 5th. Her hair is red. I am glad Mary succumbed to the craze. It is fun to have a doll around the house.

Mary kept insisting we improve the household furnishings. I bought a new hot water heater and a personal computer. The computer is the nicest piece of furniture we have in the living room. Mary still seems to want more. Fortunately, she continues to save money by being frugal. I think she went too far, however, when she spent 75 cents for a two liter bottle of de-fizzled diet Pepsi at a garage sale. Even then I didn't complain, until she served it to me.

I am still into running. I am on my third stopwatch. I inadvertently flushed the first one down the toilet when it fell off my wrist. Mary made me get rid of the second one. The alarm switch broke and every morning the alarm was going off at 5:45 AM. As for Mary's watch, she accidentally dropped it in the Atlantic Ocean last summer. I told her not to look for it. I said I would buy her another one.

This year several of us ran in the six mile race again. After the near heart attack, I am not sure Mary will let us do it again next year. It happened midway through the race when an ambulance drove up, siren blaring, and asked for Mary Young. Mary recovered when she found out Angela was okay. Angela was starting to black out after she ran the first mile. Turns out she was coming down with the flu.

Mary continues to be a good medical diagnostician. When she saw white objects in Russell's stools following a bowel movement, she correctly identified them as Styrofoam balls from the beanbags in the family room. What really impressed me, however, was when she correctly diagnosed Ryan's rash and slight fever as Lyme's disease, an newly identified ailment which can affect the nervous system and, in some cases, cause paralysis. It is transmitted to humans from diseased deer via very small ticks. A doctor confirmed Mary's diagnosis and Ryan was treated in time to prevent any problems.

Christie is a senior in high school and is busily sending in college applications. She is working part-time 30-40 hours a week at the local supermarket to earn tuition money. She discovered boys at work. One time she was parted in the driveway with a boy—"talking". Mary thought I should check on her to make sure she was okay. I told her I didn't know how to do it without looking like I was snooping. I resisted the idea of driving by on the lawn tractor. I explained to Mary that it would be hard to appear nonchalant cutting the grass at three o'clock in the morning.

This is Angela's first year in high school. She is thoroughly enjoying every minute of it. She doesn't really mind the classes, either. She plays tenor sax in three bands. Also plays soccer and softball. We had to take her to the doctor recently to have the telephone extracted from her ear. She continues to baby-sit regularly to finance her flamboyant lifestyle. Money doesn't seem to concern her. Recently, at church, she threw a twenty dollar bill into the collection basket. When asked why, she said, "That's all I had!"

Nichole is an eighth grader. She calls herself "Chef Nichole." She is always cooking sweets for Mary to eat. She takes singing, dancing, and piano. She plays softball and basketball. She is on the swimming and tennis teams. She plays French horn in the band. As a thirteen year old, two of her three personalities are great. She seems to be very ecumenical in her outlook. She often participates in the Presbyterian youth group and attends a Jewish Bar Mitzvah nearly every weekend.

Heidi is a very quiet, loud sixth grader. She is taking dancing and piano. She plays the clarinet in the band. She plays softball and basketball, is on the swim team, and is a Girl Scout. We are breaking her in as a baby-sitter. Mary had difficulty scheduling Heidi's parent-teacher conference at school, so the teachers agreed to come to our house. Mary fed them a nice lunch. After dessert, they said Heidi was a very good student.

Robert is a boy, and in the fourth grade. He plays piano and trombone, and is in baseball, basketball, and Boy Scouts. Ryan is a boy, and in the second grade. Both boys are into bicycles, accidents, soccer, and rough-housing. Robert wasn't hurt in their first bicycle collision. Ryan had to have stitches in his head after he regained consciousness. Fortunately, Ryan was not hurt as badly as the other kid in his second collision.

Marianne is five, and on top of the world. She is in kindergarten this year. One day she told me she had seen a *humongous* butterfly. I said, "Humongous?" She said, "Well, maybe it was just *big*."

Russell is three. His last haircut took about 6 weeks to complete and cost me $30, including gas. Previously he had been deathly afraid of getting haircuts. He would scream the entire time. I would physically hold him in the chair. The barber was having a nervous breakdown. We solved that with this latest haircutting approach. Mary took him in *every* day. She and the barber would ply him with candy. Then the barber would cut *one snip* of hair that day. We will probably have to give him another haircut in January *and* February. No matter what we ask him, he has the same response: "No way!"

Well, 1985 will be the year to begin lowering the budget deficit (mine; not America's). I have promised Mary we won't touch the entitlement programs, such as her long distance phone calls to North Dakota. However, our budgets for peanut butter and milk are in serious jeopardy. I am going to take a symbolic cut in my bowling budget, and drink one less beer each time.

Merry Christmas! May peace and happiness be yours in 1985.

Bob, Mary, and Family

Christmas picture 1984.

December 1985

Dear Friends,

Mary Christmas from the YOUNG'S! Mary has asked me to give you an update on our year.

The 1971 Buick wagon, at 120,000 miles, has reached a plateau in her life. She rests serenely in the driveway, complacent in the knowledge that Christie has left for college, and that Angela won't have a driver's license for a few months. Her ugly cough is gone, the result of new spark plugs. She suffers silently as the cancerous rust eats slowly away at her ponderous frame. Her pride seems undiminished despite being passed in mileage by the younger, yellow Mercedes. She knows that when it snows, she alone can make it up the steep, slippery hill to home.

This year, in New York, we had an earthquake, a hurricane, a drought, and flooding. If I see a single grasshopper (i.e. locust) next year, I plan to become a very religious person.

Christie is a freshman at Penn State, majoring in computer science. Mary and I were concerned that she would study all the time, get good grades, and be an introvert. Luckily, that didn't happen.

Angela is a sophomore in high school, majoring in music and boys. She plays the sax in the jazz band. She still loves to play the piano. She has a job at Burger King. She was named "Employee of the Month." She became upset at work one day because the bandage that had been on her hand was missing. Luckily it showed up. A customer found it in his Whopper and was nice enough to return it. Angela asked him if he wanted a replacement Whopper. He said, "No. I'm not hungry anymore."

Nichole is a freshman. She is a member of the high school swim team. She is not a good swimmer, but she enjoys the social aspect. One day she invited Mary to watch a swim meet. She told Mary to turn off at the "Grasslands exit." When I got home that night, Mary was *not* in a good mood. There *is* no Grasslands exit. Mary didn't figure that out until she reached a traffic jam just outside New York City, about 30 miles past the swim meet.

Heidi is in the seventh grade. She is our primary babysitter. She likes dancing and is taking lessons. Her dentist is happy. She decided her teeth are crooked, and she now has braces.

I have been re-doing our main bathroom. The boys have been "helping." Robert turned on the water in the tub just as the plumber was on the floor below putting in the drain. The plumber said he needed a shower anyway.

Robert is in the fifth grade. He is in all sports, and plays the trombone and piano. He is into growing.

Ryan is in the third grade. This was the first year he ran in the 6 mile race. He joined Robert, Heidi, and me. Ryan loves to play chess. I enjoyed playing with him before he started to beat me consistently.

Marianne is in the first grade. She loves life. She has very long pigtails. She can "write" letters now. I enjoyed her last letter to her friends. It went as follows:

"To Becky, i mad a lod of fres in sgool.
th prsin that moft in yr old haws is in mi clas no.
ce dosit no haw to sbel."

Translated, the letter said:

"To Becky, I made a lot of friends in school.
The person that moved in your house is in my class now.
She doesn't know how to spell."

Russell just turned four. He is asking questions constantly. Recently he asked, "Mom, what makes the Sun shine?" Mary said, "Because it is burning." He thought about that for awhile, and said, "Then where is the smoke?"

Mary's pain in her left arm and chest is starting to go away now. After suffering for three months, she went to her doctor. He seemed baffled, so we asked my brother, John, who is a doctor, for advice. John told Mary to stop carrying (22 pound) Heather in that arm.

Heather is now 18 months old, with red hair and a disposition to match. She has the lungs of an opera singer, the climbing ability of a monkey, and the appetite of a hummingbird.

Mary and Heather took a vacation to North Dakota this year for two weeks. I babysat the rest of the kids. Mary hid her keys when she left so they wouldn't get lost or stolen. They did not get stolen. We are still looking for them.

Well, we are all looking forward to a happy and relaxing 1986. May your year be the same!

Bob, Mary, and Family

Christmas picture 1985.

December 1986

Dear Friends,

Merry Christmas from the YOUNG'S! Mary again asked me to write my annual epistle.

I'm sure you will be delighted to hear that the 1971 Buick station wagon is still a contributing member of the family. While the younger, yellow Mercedes rests comfortably in the garage, having just passed the 140,000 mile mark, the green Buick, her personality permanently changed following transplants of a starter motor, water pump, and brake master cylinder, continues to brave life outside, like an old dog, subjected to heat, rain, and cold. Her ponderous, rusty, partially mangled body rests quietly in the driveway, oil and anti-freeze dripping continuously from open sores on her diseased underside. Her spirit lies dormant in that massive frame until, at last, she feels the impatient foot of 16-year-old Angela urging her on. Then together they flit recklessly down the road, oblivious to danger: one too old to care; the other too young to know.

I think Mary is getting soft in her hold age. Late the other night, long after dinner was over, she said "yes" when Robert came and asked if he could have a crust of bread.

Mary is trying to lose weight though hypnosis. It hasn't worked yet, however. Every time she listens to the tape and the hypnotist says "Close your eyes and go to sleep", Mary closes her eyes and goes to sleep. The problem is that her snoring drowns out the voice of the hypnotist.

We did a lot of traveling this year. Robert, Ryan, Heidi, and I went to Washington DC and Atlantic City with Jack, Betty, Brian, and Andrea Payne. Now I know why people always wear hats on the Atlantic City boardwalk. The kids thought it was really funny when a seagull dropped a load on my head.

Mary and I went to Maine and Plymouth, Massachusetts with her parents. We made a dent in the lobster population. Later Mary and her folds toured the Amish settlements in Pennsylvania after they drove Christie to college.

Christie is a sophomore at Penn State. She still loves college and is working harder this year. She observed that Mary and I are getting smarter as she grows older.

We now have "cash banking" in our home. Angela has a part time waitressing job. She comes home with her pockets stuffed with tip money.

Nichole died and went to heaven. She made the cheerleading squad.

It is Heidi's year for braces, bar mitzvahs, and babysitting. Mary and I are worried about her development. She has turned 13, and is still a pleasant person.

We are trying to break-in Robert as a babysitter. He has trouble concentrating, so we pay Marianne to remind him that he is babysitting. He also has been earning money cutting the neighbors lawn, and raking leaves with Ryan. I do my own yard. I can't afford their rates.

Ryan stays busy with piano, saxophone, scouts, baseball, soccer, basketball, and chess. He is learning humility. I beat him twice in chess.

This is Marianne's first year of soccer. She has a good attitude. Following a 4 to 1 defeat, she mused, "Gee, we would have tied them if that one kid hadn't scored those three goals!"

Russell is attending nursery school this year. Mary thought we had better start early with him. She thinks he is stubborn; I think he is principled. He is still dad's helper. Whenever I come home from work he says, "What are we going to fix tonight, Dad?"

Heather is 2 and 1/2 now. She is not a quiet or bashful person. She can be very persuasive. I think she is going to be a politician. The other night in church, she told me she had to go potty. I told her to wait until the service was over. About 5 minutes later she came and whispered in my ear, "Dad, I am going to poop my pants!" Needless to say, I took her out immediately.

I ran in the New York Marathon this year (26 miles). I finished in five hours. When people asked why I did it, I said, "Because it felt so good when I stopped!"

The entire family was the finale for the school talent show. We sang "So Long, Farewell" from the Sound of Music movie. During the performance, Heather spontaneously started to dance, the crowd got the giggles, and then we got the giggles. The singing kept degenerating until, by the middle of the song, no one could sing any more. People loved it!

Well, in summary, it's been a pretty good year. We were not wiped out in a nuclear war, and the kids had very few colds.

Mary peace and happiness be yours in 1987!

Bob, Mary,
    Christie (19), Angela (16), Nichole (15),
        Heidi (13), Robert (12), Ryan (9),
            Marianne (7), Russell (5), and Heather (2)

Christmas picture 1986.

Bob and Mary December 1986.

This is me before my first New York Marathon in November of 1986. At the age of 43, I was in the best shape of my life.

Here I am after I completed the five hour run. I was happy to be alive and happy that it was over.

Here is a blurry photo of the Young Family singers. Notice in the second photo that Heather on the far left is doing her spontaneous dance and circling around the rest of the group. The entire audience was laughing uncontrollably, as were we.

The Young Family Singers - Before

The Young Family Singers - After (note Heather)

December 1987

Dear Friends,

Merry Christmas from the YOUNG'S! Mary suggested that I give you a brief summary of the year's events.

The 1971 green Buick Estate station wagon died a violent death on a cold, dark night last winter, a victim of treacherous black ice and a stubborn tree. She died valiantly. Her last act, as she careened out of control, was to use her bulky frame to shield her young driver, Angela, and passenger, Robert. It was with a great deal of sadness that I paid the $100 to have her lifeless hulk taken away. At times, when I think of her loyalty, and, let me say it, GUTS, tears well up in my eyes. The only thing that keeps me going is the conviction that she is now riding that tranquil highway in the sky, free of rust and safe from mechanical failure.

Her successor is a nondescript 1979 Olds Delta 88 with 88,000 miles. While the replacement has less character than her predecessor, she does seem to have a resiliency not unlike the Buick. Reinforced by $1,000 worth of repairs, the Olds is still intact in spite of her three teenage drivers: Christie, Angela, and Nichole.

The senior member of the fleet is now the 1976 Yellow Mercedes, with 157,000 miles. I was starting to think of this car as *old*, until a business associate pointed out that I owned a "*classic.*" I now feel "cool" since I own an "antique" Mercedes.

Speaking of old, Mary and I celebrated our twentieth anniversary by taking a two week vacation in Hawaii last winter. I had flown enough on Northwest Airlines to qualify for free tickets. We arrived home to find that our babysitters, Mary's Mom and Dad, had survived.

I've heard that you lose your hair after you turn 40. That's not really true. I admit that my hairline is rapidly receding, but to compensate, the hair in my nose and ears seems to be growing out of control. I don't know if the hairline is a factor or not, but Mary recently observed that I have a pointy head. I'm not sure I should have encouraged her to get new contact lenses.

I suspect Mary may be aging. Recently I asked her, "Is it true that when you get old the first thing to go is your memory?" She said, "I don't remember."

Christie (20) is a junior at Penn State. She hasn't flunked out yet. She is studying business logistics. I don't know exactly what that is, but she tells me she has to join the Teamsters Union to get a job.

Angela (17) is a senior in high school. We couldn't understand why she got so excited when we gave her a set of car keys for Christmas, until we realized that she thought we had bought her a car!

Nichole (16) came up with the most creative way to waste energy. While it is customary in this house to have all the lights on, and, in the winter, the doors open, the other day in her room I found both the humidifier and the dehumidifier running at the same time, one putting moisture into the air, the other taking it out!

Heidi (14) is enjoying her first year of high school. We get to use the phone when she goes to the bathroom.

"Old" is "in" this year. Nichole and Heidi went to Greenwich Village in New York City and bought used wool car-coats for $8 apiece. Heidi then doubled her cost by spending $8 to get hers cleaned. Nichole didn't bother.

Robert just became a teenager (13). His hairline seems to be moving towards his eyebrows. If it doesn't stop pretty quickly, he won't have a forehead. In any case, the girls seem attracted by this phenomenon.

Ryan (10) was altar boy for a wedding recently. Immediately before the ceremony, the groom gave him an envelope containing a gratuity. Lacking the sensitivity to open it later, Ryan ripped the card open and found a $20 bill. Surprised to find that much, he turned to the groom and asked, "Did you want some change?"

Marianne (8) loves dancing and soccer. She seems to think there is a strong similarity between the two activities, much to the dismay of her dancing partners.

Russell (6) is in kindergarten. He hasn't changed; he still asks a lot of questions. Recently he said, "Dad, what is under the United States?" I told him to ask his mother. Another time, when Mary's Mom was here, she asked him if he wanted some extra cake frosting. He said, "No, but save it for my mom. She is on a diet and will eat it later."

Heather (3) just had her long red hair cut. She looks different now, but acts the same. She makes Hulk Hogan, the professional wrestler, seem like a wimp. Her favorite sayings this year were "I can't know" and "awesome." She has reached the age of independence. She can now open the refrigerator door.

May you have a joyful year in 1988!

Bob, Mary, and Family

Christmas picture 1987.

Mary and Bob in Hawaii in 1987. We had this picture taken when we attended a Luau.

November 1988

Dear Friends,

Merry Christmas from the YOUNG'S! Mary asked me to write you a short, personalized form letter.

Mary's body continues to be a medical marvel. In June she had a rib removed which contained an aggressive tumor. Luckily it was benign. Prior to the operation, she had so many X-rays that she glowed in the dark. Anyway, she is fine now. To celebrate her recover, we had friends over for a rib dinner.

Before Mary went to the hospital, the local priest called to find out what was going on. He had heard a rumor that she might be ill. Then when he observed Angela, Nichole, and Heidi attending daily Mass, he concluded things must be pretty bad. Mary had to explain that Angela was going to church as a punishment from us, and that Nichole and Heidi were going because they wanted a ride to school. They hate to take the bus!

Mary was confused about who to vote for this year in the Presidential election. I told her that if she wanted to vote liberal, she should vote for Dukakis, the guy in the commercial driving the army tank; and that if she wanted to vote conservative, she should vote for Bush, the guy who was proposing the child care giveaway program.

Mary has been very frustrated because several neighbors "walk" their dogs along our property. She wanted to erect a sign saying, "Please walk your dog elsewhere. My children play here and get dog doo-doo all over themselves, which is very unsanitary and messy." I told her we should just have a sign which said, "NO DOGSHITTING ALLOWED". We compromised and put up a professionally painted sign with a big red X covering the image of a dog pooping.

Christie (21) will be graduating from Penn State this year. She had a real good job in the city with Citibank last summer, and commuted by train into Grand Central Station every day. She is not the best commuter yet. Twice on the way home she fell asleep and rode the train to the end of the line.

Angela (18) is in Mexico for a year on a student exchange program. Mary asked her to write often. After four weeks without a letter, we finally called her. She was fine, but lonesome. Turns out she had written every day, but hadn't mailed the loooooong letter! She is learning to speak Spanish, eat Tacos with lots of onions for breakfast, dance Mexican style, and cohabitate with friendly lizards. She has to work on Spanish more. One day she thought she said, "I was very scared." But her friends explained that she had said, "I had a lot of shit."

Nichole (17) is busy finishing up her senior year in high school and investigating colleges. She was ready to mail letters to eight colleges when I happened to notice that she was asking each of the eight schools to send her an "aplication".

Heidi (15) is a sophomore. She is still taking school seriously, and loves her Art course. Her social agenda has expanded dramatically, however. Last year we worried about her because she was still a very pleasant and respectful teenager. We have stopped worrying.

Robert (14) has been making money cutting the neighbors' lawn. One day Ryan came screaming, "Dad! Hurry and come! Rob needs you right away!" I ran over, expecting to see Rob on the ground bleeding to death. Instead, I saw the neighbors' dog going crazy as his long leash rope slowly disappeared into the rotating mower blades pulling the terrified dog with it. My quick move to the "OFF" switch kept that dog from becoming a doggie-burger. Later I realized that if I had been a little slower, I might not have needed the dog doo-doo sign. Robert is getting as frugal as his mother, now that he has to buy his own clothes. He discovered that his socks will last twice as long if he turns them upside down when they get holes.

Ryan (11) is rapidly becoming our main baby-sitter. He loves to earn money so he can spend it all on baseball cards. He plays baseball and basketball. He plays sax in the jazz band and plays the piano. I recently asked him, "What is your favorite activity?" He quickly responded, "Lunch!"

Marianne (9) will probably be a counselor when she grows up. I took a college writing course last winter. Marianne observed my obvious disappointment when I got my grade and it was only a "B". She came up to me, patted me on the back, and said, "That's okay, Dad. A "B" is better than a "C"."

Russell (7) is in the first grade. We asked his teacher how he was doing in school. She said, "Fine, except when he makes noises during class." He wanted to know how the doctors removed Mary's rib. I said, "With a saw." He said, "Do you mean a chain saw?"

Heather (4) does a good job surviving despite all the comings and goings of the older people in the house. Mary and I vacationed for a week last winter, and left Angela to babysit. A friend dropped by to check up on things. Heather answered the door, took her hand, whispered "I want to show you something", and led her upstairs to our room. Then, in the manner of a museum curator giving guided tours, pointed to our bed and said very calmly, "My Mom and Dad used to live here."

Heather's Uncle noticed her banging her head against the couch. He said, "Don't do that. You might get brain damage!" Heather responded, "Why? Is that what happened to you?"

I ran the New York Marathon again this year, and finished. My kids were impressed until they found out that at 21 miles a one-legged man with crutches passed me; at 22 miles a midget passed me; and at 23 miles a man with no legs and hands passed me in a wheelchair.

I have read that, as couples get older, their ardor for one another often remains undiminished. I have decided that one contributing factor could be bifocals. Each spouse can actually see one another clearly both far and near!

May you have a fulfilling year in 1989!

Bob, Mary, and Family

Christmas picture 1988.

December 1989

Dear Friends,

Merry Christmas from the YOUNG'S! Mary suggested I give you a personal update on recent happenings.

We were really lucky this year: while we didn't win the million dollar lottery, we didn't lose a million dollars either!

Mary continues to watch her weight and fight the aging process. She belongs to an exercise class, plus she walks 30 minutes every morning. I observed that her appetite seems to be stimulated by all the exercise; but she claims the added pounds are caused by the fat turning to muscle.

I jogged again this year to control my weight, culminating this fall with my fourth New York City Marathon. I beat my previous best time by 10 minutes because my brother, John, running his first marathon, told me jokes the last 8 miles to take my mind off the race.

While my body is getting better, my mind seems less stable. It is harder to adapt to change. For example, the other day Mary put the ironing board *away*, and when I came home from work I suddenly became disoriented.

I am still a pretty good handyman around the house, but sometimes Mary has to encourage me. I got frustrated trying to fix the dryer, so I told her to buy a new one. Instead, Mary enlisted the help of a neighbor and found the screws holding the cover. Then I was able to remove the cover and replace the $12 belt inside.

You are probably wondering about my cars. The nondescript 1979 Brown Olds has just passed the 100,000 mile mark. Luckily every time Nichole hit something it tended to be a "glancing blow." Despite having traveled 173,000 miles over the last 13 years, the loyal 1976 yellow Mercedes is still with us. I had a lapse in judgment and tried to sell her for $3,000. Fortunately there were no buyers. Since then she has been hit three times, and we have collected $2,700 in insurance. She seems to gracefully accept my decision to keep the dents *and* the money.

Christie (22) graduated from Penn State this year and GOT A JOB with a company called Ciba-Geigy. She couldn't understand why I was ecstatic. I explained that if she hadn't been hired by a some employer, she would have had to stay at home, her self esteem would have dropped, she would have gotten lazy and fat, she would have become ill and depressed, and ultimately she would have become a burden the rest of her life to me and society. She rented the basement bedroom from us prior to moving into her own apartment this month. She didn't spend a great deal of time keeping her room clean. Mary and I are now trying to devise ways to destroy the organisms that invaded her room during her tenure.

Angela (19) came home from her year in Mexico, and is now attending her first year of college at the State University in Binghamton, NY. Mary and I visited her in Mexico last winter. Angela gave us the tour of all the places to eat in Minatitlan and demonstrated how she gained 26 pounds on Mexican food. This summer after returning, she decided she wanted to be treated as an adult, so I started charging her rent for room and board.

Nichole (18) is doing really well now. Right after I wrote last year, she was in a car accident and broke her jaw, nose, ribs, and sustained facial cuts. Her attitude was great throughout the whole ordeal, and she has healed miraculously. She graduated from high school this year, and is now attending the State University at Albany, NY. She has been away from home long enough to conclude her parents are getting smarter. She talks about us to her friends. I heard her on the phone describing Mary and me to a new boyfriend. She said, "With her new haircut, Mom looks like Dr. Spock on Star Trek. Dad looks like Grandpa on the 'Munsters'."

Heidi (16) is a junior in high school. She has been working hard and saving her money for college. Starting this year, she has her OWN bedroom. She asked me if she could paint her room. I said, "Sure. Why not?" Now one entire wall is a mural of a beach scene. I am teaching her to drive. She makes me nervous when she says, "Am I on the right side of the road?" Or "I forget which pedal is the brake!"

Robert (15) is recovering nicely from the broken femur sustained while playing soccer with a friend. He maintained his spirits extremely well during his 7 weeks in traction in the hospital, his 6 weeks in a body cast, and several weeks on crutches. His friends kept him supplied with pizza and friendship during his hospital stay. They would get admitted to his room by claiming they were a brother or sister. One day he had thirteen brothers and sisters in his room, all 14 years old! He still limps, but has recovered well enough to play tennis and golf, and make the freshman soccer team.

Ryan (12) is eating and growing. He eats like a snake: just swallows everything whole and then absorbs it. Girls started calling him when school started this year, then they stopped. Mary asked, "What happened?" He said, "I told them not to call anymore unless they had something to say." He made the traveling basketball team this year, and the All-Star baseball team. I also took him golfing. I was delighted at the end when I asked him, "How many balls did you lose?" and he said, "None." But then he continued, "I did lose a three-wood and a nine-iron."

Marianne (10) is in the fifth grade. Her love is soccer. When you watch her game, you just look for the ball and know there will be a streak of long hair nearby. Her job at home is to wipe off the table and vacuum the floor after dinner. Needless to say, the ants are well-fed. She is very helpful around the house, although she could listen more closely to directions. Mary asked her and Robert to put a pan of steaming hot water in the chest style freezer to defrost it. Later Mary discovered the miscommunication when she asked Marianne how the project was progressing, and Marianne said, "Great! We have it about half-full already."

Russell (8) is in the second grade. Recently at the breakfast table I asked, "What makes you so good looking?" To which he replied, "Years of practice!" Every Saturday he and Heather use all the chairs, cushions, sleeping bags, and other loose objects to make a "fort." Lately he has found my workbench, and is building things with wood. It there was an award for "Most Creative Play", he would get it.

Heather (5) is in kindergarten this year. Mary showed her how to pray to Saint Anthony one day when she lost something. Recently, when she lost something else, she said, "Maybe Saint Anthony took it again!" As the youngest of nine, she has learned to survive. She will NOT "inherit the earth"!

People think the earth is getting warmer due to the impact of fluorocarbons on the ozone layer. Every parent knows better. It is from their kids collectively leaving doors open in the winter.

We took a family weekend vacation in Plymouth, Massachusetts. We saw Plymouth Rock, toured a replica of the Mayflower, and visited a village simulating the first settlement in the United States. The kids loved the indoor swimming pool at the motel, and eating Dunkin Donuts for breakfast.

This has been an interesting year. The Berlin Wall has become dysfunctional, the Japanese bought Rockefeller Center, and Mary can do volunteer work now that all the kids are in school. Mary also convinced me that we should take a course on "How to Raise Kids." The kids think it may be too late, but history shows that strange things can happen!

May you have a delightful decade!

Bob, Mary, and Family

Christmas picture 1989.

Robert A. Young

December 1990

Dear Friends,

Merry Christmas from the YOUNG'S! Mary asked me to chronicle the annual happenings as a record for posterity.

This year will never be forgotten. Against the wishes of my lovely wife, I removed the fountain from the backyard. Mary always saw the fountain as a lovely colored centerpiece for future wedding receptions. I saw it as a Machiavellian device designed to consume labor and money. After two different contractors came to remove the fountain and abandoned the job, I, "Rambo", decided to do the job myself. I rented a 100 pound jackhammer, attacked the reinforced concrete, and discovered my physical limitations. Mary finally got Rob out of school early so he could help me. That simple little act saved my life. She also wrote a nice letter to the neighbors explaining that the reason we ran the jackhammer at 6 AM the next morning was so that we didn't have to pay another day's rent of $180.

Mary did talk me into replacing a couple of worn doors in the house after Christmas last year. Once I agreed, she said we might as well do fourteen of them, replace all the wood trim upstairs, sand and varnish the hardwood floors, remove the wallpaper, patch and paint the walls and ceilings, remove paint from 12 windows and stain and varnish them, replace the hall carpeting, and put in some drapes. I think by next Easter we will be nearly done. She mentioned we may want to patch the hole in the kitchen wall next . . . One side benefit of doing Robert's room was that we discovered what was causing the smell: an uneaten lunch he had stored in his closet several months earlier.

This was also the year of deer ticks and Lyme's disease. Both Mary and Nichole had it. Nichole had it so bad one side of her face was paralyzed for a couple of weeks. She couldn't even blink her eye or move her mouth. We really laughed. She looked so funny. Mary found 13 ticks on Heather one day. We're convinced that is a World's Record.

The nondescript 1979 Oldsmobile Delta 88 I bought in 1987 is no longer with us. She has joined the 1971 Green Buick in the Hereafter for cars. It wasn't Nichole's fault, and no one was hurt. Despite serving us for 20,000 miles, none of us were emotionally attached to the Olds, like we were with the 1971 Buick. I think part of it was that we CHOSE the Buick, and spent 16 years with her through thick and thin, whereas our relationship with the Olds was more one of convenience. She was just there when we needed her. But she was only with us three years, and had never become a PART of the family. Her replacement is a 1979 Ford T-Bird with 82,000 miles.

We did our share of traveling this year. Mary and I spent two weeks in Europe. We visited Germany, Austria, France, and Switzerland. We rented a car and sped around the Autobahn. Then our entire family went to North Dakota for three weeks to encounter our 'roots'. I made two trips to California to visit my brother. Mary traveled to Montana to attend a wedding. The good news is that all our airline tickets were free, compliments of my frequent flyer points from work-related travel.

During the time Mary was gone in August, I had to do the shopping alone. I didn't realize it was possible to spend $100 on milk, cereal, and hot dogs. The kids got hyper they ate so much sugared cereal.

Mary loves to pray the Rosary. One day she was praying so hard in the car she didn't notice right away that she was speeding past a cop. Luckily he didn't stop her. Perhaps he was busy saying HIS Rosary!

Christie (23) is still working for Ciba-Geigy in New Jersey. Luckily she got a raise so she could continue buying nylons. She hates to wash the used ones. She moved home for a month when she was between roommates and apartments. When she moved out again she left behind some furniture for the "Young's Warehouse."

Angela (20) is attending her second year of college at the State University in Binghamton, NY. She is majoring in Music. She made the "crew" (rowing) team. The team is terrible but she is having a ball. She was the Music Director for a summer youth camp. We were all proud of her.

Nichole (19) is attending her second year of college at the State University in Albany, NY. She is majoring in sorority, boys, and communications (telephone). When her checks started bouncing last year, I asked, "Didn't you balance your checkbook?" She replied, "What does that mean?"

Heidi (17) is a senior, studying hard, getting ready for college, and in a million activities. She has been giving her time helping the homeless and visiting old people. (We may have a Mother Teresa on our hands.) She continues to have a strong interest in Art. She designed a symbol that the local United Way is using for its Youth Leadership program.

Robert (16) is a sophomore, and keeps very busy. He studies hard and mercilessly hounds his teachers for grades. In August he started as a waiter at Friendlys, with no training. He has set a new 'service' standard, requiring three separate trips to the table to deliver coffee, cream, and saucer. He is into soccer, lacrosse, weightlifting, girls, and music. He bought a new stereo and is in seventh heaven. It barely fits in his room.

Ryan (13) is in the eighth grade. His braces have not slowed him down since he does not use his teeth to eat. He likes sports, music, and arguing. However, the other day he mused philosophically, "Arguing with Mom is like arguing with an umpire. You can't win!"

While golfing one day with Robert and Ryan, I was explaining how we were enjoying a rare moment: perfect weather, delightful sport, great relationships . . . I said, "It just doesn't get any better than this!" Then Rob asked, "You mean this is even better than sex?" I responded quickly, "It lasts longer."

Marianne (11) is in the sixth grade. She is becoming our regular babysitter. She loves soccer and is doing well with piano. She is now in Middle School (junior high), and is enjoying her 'freedom'. She has her own locker. She no longer has to walk in straight lines. Really! How much better could it be?

Russell (9) is in the third grade. He has been taking speech lessons and now talks better that the rest of the family. He loves to design and build helicopters and cars with his Construx set. He played baseball last summer. Luckily, not too many balls were hit to right field since he was playing in the dirt most of the time.

Heather (6) is in the first grade. On her last report card the teacher indicated, "*We* are working on not always having to be 'first'." I am surprised that a teacher would want to be 'first' all the time.

Heather does worry about others. Last summer she said, "Mom, I think you should tell Russell to come in from the street now. I know you don't like to be disturbed during your nap, and if he gets run over by a car, you will be disturbed."

Heather still loves to eat, and can get creative when necessary. When Mary told her and Russell they couldn't have seconds, Heather said, "Can't we just eat the crumbs off the table?"

World events have been nothing short of incredible this year. Germany has been reunited. The Russian Empire is disintegrating. Bush has sent five hundred thousand troops to help Saudi Arabia stop Saddam Hussein, and get Iraq out of Kuwait. Margaret Thatcher lost her job. Jesse Jackson didn't run for anything. I shot a 92 in golf. The 1976 Mercedes is still going strong after 180,000 miles. Mary took the ironing board down.

May you have a fun 1991!

Bob, Mary, and Family

Christmas picture 1990 taken at the wedding in North Dakota.

Pictures of the fountain before and after the demolition, and me as Rambo!

The fountain before

The demolisher

The fountain after demolition

December 1991

Dear Friends,

Merry Christmas from the YOUNG'S! Mary asked me to relate the highlights of the year.

Mary and I celebrated our 25th wedding anniversary this year. The kids, led by Angela, arranged for a special Mass to renew our wedding vows, followed by a reception. Every one of the kids participated in the Mass in some way. Our parents came to the Mass and reception. Mary and I were really touched by the whole experience. Now we're looking forward to our fiftieth!

Earlier, in April, Mary and I went to Hawaii for our "honeymoon", compliments of my frequent flyer programs. I surprised Mary by getting First Class tickets. It took her awhile to understand what was happening when we got on the airplane. She looked back into the coach section and asked, "Why are those seats back there SO SMALL?"

Mary's life has changed a lot. With three kids in college, we only have five at home now during the school year. And they are in school all day. She was really excited the other day when I came home from work. She exclaimed, "There was only ONE unmatched sock in the wash this week!"

Mary is still "busy", but she spends a lot more time doing things she enjoys: church every day, phoning relatives, PTA, Parish Council, crafts, Bible Study, ironing, etc.

The Mercedes is still alive . . . but I'm not sure for how long. I noticed a new dent the other night when I came home from work. When I asked Mary about it, she said, "I hit the van when I backed out of the garage because I wanted to make sure I didn't hit your perfectly trimmed bushes!"

Christie (24) is living in New Jersey and working for Ciba-Geigy. Christie is living the American dream: she is maxed out on all her credit cards! Christie traveled with Mary and me to Chicago for Nancy Moen's wedding. The wedding and trip were wonderful!

Angela (21) is in her third year at the State University in Binghamton, NY. This year she made a religious pilgrimage to Medjugorje, Yugoslavia. She had some incredibly great experiences and came back with a wonderfully fresh perspective of herself and a strong commitment to her faith.

Nichole (20) is a junior at the State University in Albany. She is living off campus this year with several friends. She is treasurer of her sorority . . . (scary isn't it!). I was very worried about her grades last year and told her if she got straight "A's", I would buy her a car. I knew that would be impossible. She scared the heck out of me by getting "A's" in every subject but one. I'll never do THAT again!

Heidi (18) graduated from high school this year and is now attending the State University in Binghamton. At a ceremony last spring she received several awards. The most meaningful was the "Outstanding Senior Girl" award which is decided by a vote of the senior class and school faculty. Thereafter, Mary and I introduced ourselves at all school functions as "Heidi's parents". Sometimes Heidi "forgets" things. She went into

New York City one day, and when she returned 8 hours later found her car in the train station parking lot with the engine still running.

Robert (17) is a junior in high school. He is on the Lacrosse team. That is a game whereby you wear a helmet and gloves and run around a field hitting each other with big sticks under the pretense that you are trying to catch a little rubber ball. Rob just got his driver's license (on the second try). He failed his first test when he cut in front of an oncoming car and nearly caused an accident. The instructor had Rob pull over immediately and screamed, "You failed the test and YOU ALMOST KILLED US!"

Ryan (14) graduated from the eighth grade and is now a freshman in high school. Last spring I drove him to the annual dance, a semi-formal occasion. I asked him, "Why are you wearing SHORTS to a semi-formal?" He replied, "Why not? It's really warm tonight." He hasn't started to date yet.

Marianne (12) is in the seventh grade. She is pretty well healed now. She had a bike accident and used her face as a brake. In school, she was selected to be in the premier singing group. Although she is still twelve, Mary and I think she acts like a teenager already.

Russell (10) is in the fourth grade. He told me he wants to be a sled inventor when he grows up. I asked him how he was doing at school. He said, "I'm an average normal." I was upstairs the other day and heard a loud crash. It was a window being broken. I looked outside and saw Russell and screamed, "What did you do?" He said, "I threw a rock and hit the window." I said, "Why did you do that?" He replied, "I didn't notice that the house was there."

Heather (7) is in the second grade. She has already established herself as a terror on the soccer field. After every game we hear comments from the sideline. "Did you see that redhead out there knocking those boys around?" The other day her fish died. I asked her how she felt. She said, "I'm kind of glad. I was writing a story about the fish and now I have an ending!"

Well, in summary, the year of our Silver wedding anniversary has been very enjoyable and fulfilling. Mary and I have really had an opportunity to enjoy our kids and our respective families this year. As they say in the beer commercial, "It just doesn't get any better than this!" Buurrppp.

Have a happy and Holy 1992!

Bob, Mary, and Family

Christmas picture 1991.

December 1992

Dear Friends,

Merry Christmas from the YOUNGs! Mary has again asked that I send you our annual update.

Well, I decided I am married to a saint. Mary prays, and God answers her prayers. She prayed for me to become more spiritual, and then ZAP, it hit me! It took a great deal of perseverance on her part; she had been praying for 25 years.

As a result, the family started a Sunday night prayer group at the church, and is now committed to having God ZAP others. Our perspectives have really been changing.

I used to avoid funerals. Now my attitude is different. Recently a friend said, "Thanks for coming to my father's funeral." I responded, "No problem. I enjoyed it!"

Rob put a bumper sticker on his old Ford, which says, "The angels are watching over me." Mary, Heather, and Rob were in the car when it stalled on the railroad track. They looked and saw a train bearing down on them. Suddenly, inexplicably, the car moved forward off the track! This is just one of the many miracles we have experienced recently.

The big family event this year was DISNEYWORLD. Mary has had a dream for the last 10 years of going there as a FAMILY. Well, we did it! All eleven of us. We drove straight though, coming and going. We gorged ourselves on the rides for six straight days, running from one to another, from morning to night. We definitely got our money's worth! We experienced several family bonding moments. One was on the way home in the van after we had all over-eaten some gas-inducing food.

We had a "baby" for several months this year. Felicia was born in prison, and had lived there with her mother for 18 months until the authorities said she had to leave. She stayed with us until her mother got out on parole. She was really delightful to have; the kids enjoyed playing with her. Occasionally her mother brings her up from the city to visit us now.

Heather (8) is in the third grade. Last spring she found a large cardboard box, made it into a bed, put it in the kitchen, and then proceeded to sleep in it every night. Mary and I were concerned about what she might tell her schoolmates and teacher . . . "I sleep in a cardboard box in the kitchen. . . ."

Russell (11) is in the fifth grade. He complained to Mary of having a pain "down under where the sun doesn't shine". He had to have a hernia operation the day after Thanksgiving last fall.

Marianne (13) is a typical 13-year-old. Good and bad; good and bad; good and bad. She just got her braces for her teeth. She is great for giving HUGS. She is in the eighth grade, and on the traveling soccer team. She has made a lot of new friends this year. She gives her dad credit for being ZAPPED with the Holy Spirit, and changing her life.

Ryan (15) is a sophomore in high school. He has had his share of miracles. He prayed for a ski jacket, and the Lord had someone give him $120 anonymously. Needless to say, he was a little excited. His grades have been quite good lately. Last spring I told him I would let him buy a Nintendo game if his grades were high enough. Much to his surprise, and mine, he succeeded.

Robert (18) is a senior in high school. His volunteer work keeps him very busy: helping the mentally handicapped, visiting the sick and elderly, and collecting food for the homeless. He also spent a week with the Glenmary Missionaries in Kentucky. Despite his opinion to the contrary, Robert is still not perfect, however. He hit a stalled car on the highway and was unsuccessful in convincing me that it wasn't his fault. Then later he got a speeding ticket. I took his driver's license away for life.

Heidi (19) is a sophomore at the State University in Binghamton, NY. She is majoring in Art, and doing well. She made a pilgrimage to Scottsdale Arizona and came back filled with the Holy Spirit. She is now spreading the Gospel at college, in her own quiet way.

Nichole (21) is a senior at the State University in Albany, NY. She is doing amazingly well in her classes, despite being President of her Sorority. She bought Christie's old car, so now is quite independent. She and a friend had some excitement while they were camping out in a cabin. They started a fire in the "stove", and realized later when the room filled with smoke that they had started a fire in the oven!

Angela (22) is a senior at the State University in Binghamton, NY. Following her religious pilgrimage to Medjugorje last year, she "freaked out on religion" before I did, and kept giving me books to read which ultimately resulted in me being zapped. This year she made a pilgrimage to Scottsdale Arizona. She and Tim, her boyfriend, started a prayer group at college, and are really having an impact on others.

Christie (25) is doing well. She is still living in New Jersey and working for Ciba-Geigy. She bought her first BRAND NEW car! She is living the life of a yuppie (young unmarried professional). We were delighted when she was able to come to Disneyworld with us, and re-live her role as the oldest "child" and chief baby-sitter. I think that, due to this trip, she decided to put off any thoughts of marriage and children for another decade.

Well, in summary, it's been a growing year for our family, and I believe this is just the beginning.

May you and your family have a happy and holy 1993!

Bob, Mary, and Family

Christmas picture 1992.

December 1993

Dear Friends,

Merry Christmas from the YOUNG's! Mary asked me to convey the annual family highlights.

It was an unbelievable year. We swam in an ocean of God's blessings.

The big event was Angela's wedding. She is now Mrs. Angela Lock! Angela, Tim, and the Holy Spirit orchestrated an uplifting, spirit-filled ceremony. Mary outdid herself by making a zillion arrangements, including a joyous reception. Tim and Angela are now living in Binghamton, where Tim is attending graduate school and Angela is working as a youth minister.

Mary and I vacationed in Rome and attended a general papal audience at the Vatican, thanks to Father Gene Reyes, a dear friend. Father arranged for us to have front-row seats. Pope John Paul II held our hands, visited with us briefly, put his hand on my head and blessed our family, and gave us each a rosary. WOW! As he walked away, my knees just folded I was so overcome with emotion. Mary was so excited she glowed like a light bulb.

Ryan and Marianne traveled to Denver in August to see the Pope and attend World Youth Day. They traveled via bus from Ohio with over 500 other kids and several very spiritual Friars. The young Friars really impressed the kids with their commitment to following the way of Christ, living the virtues of poverty, chastity, and obedience. It was a life-changing experience for both Ryan and Marianne.

Heidi, Nino (her boyfriend), Angela, Tim, Mary, and I all graduated from the 'International School for Catholic Lay Evangelists'. We each attended a one-week class in Pensacola, Florida. The school is the first of its kind. It emphasizes the fundamentals of the faith in a very enlightening way, and shows how to spread the "good news" through personal witness.

Robert graduated from high school and is attending the Franciscan University of Steubenville, in Ohio. He LOVES it. He is letting the Light shine through. With respect to his driving, he had more accidents. They weren't his fault; people keep stopping in front of him. He also ran into the wall of the garage and shattered the windshield of the Mercedes. I agreed with him that it was my mistake for expecting him to drive that car into the garage.

Ryan just got his driver's license yesterday. He hasn't had any accidents yet. He has several jobs. He is a waiter and fountain person at Friendly's, a sports counselor, a mower of lawns, a baby-sitter, and a part-time receptionist. He is having a great time in his high school ethics class; he is emerging as the 'resident philosopher'. Perhaps his middle name of 'Paul' is prophetic.

Rob and Ryan, against the advice of their parents, celebrated the Fourth of July by setting off fireworks in a nearby nature preserve. They are now on probation, following their arrest and sentencing. The arresting policeman was not in a real good mood after chasing them on foot through the woods, and then by car to our house. His frustration peaked when he got into his patrol car to take the hand-cuffed boys to the police station, and Ryan said, "Could you put on my seat belt? My mother says I must always use one."

Marianne is a freshman in high school. She is a real 'jock'. She plays on the field hockey team and on the soccer team. Her team carried her off the field on their shoulders when she scored the winning goal in the last field hockey game of the season. Coming back from her Denver pilgrimage, she had an asthma attack, lost consciousness in the bus, and was taken by ambulance to a hospital. She was surprised and gratified to discover that when Ryan realized she might die, he acted concerned!

Russell is a sixth-grader. He has some close friends that play together, doing what boys that age like to do. If you have read the book "Huckleberry Finn", then you have an idea of his lifestyle. He joined the Boy Scouts, and recently went on his first camping trip. He walked five miles to the campsite with his sleeping bag and knapsack. Before the trip, I gave him some helpful advice about packing. We shed about 30 pounds of weight by leaving behind an extra pair of shoes, 3 extra sets of clothes, 4 extra knives, and 3 large hard-bound books . . . . (he hates to read!). Russell continues to be creative. I asked him why the electric pencil sharpener was in the back yard, and he said, "I used it to sharpen my home-made arrows."

Heather is 9, and in the fourth grade. She is on the girls 'traveling' soccer team and thoroughly enjoys it. She has no fear! Shortly she will want braces for her teeth, like all the other kids her age. I want to wait until she gets older to ensure that she will have teeth to brace! She helped Russell and me build a tree house, using an electric saw and an electric drill. Despite that, she still has all her fingers which she uses adroitly for her art projects.

Nichole graduated from the University of Albany this year, and is working as a financial planner. She is living life to the fullest, rooming with her college girl friend and driving her new car (only two speeding tickets in 3 months . . .). The police caught a thief as he was leaving their apartment with his loot. Nothing in his bag belonged to Nichole; she didn't have anything worth stealing!

Christie continues to 'move up' in the business world. She accepted a position with a fast-growing company and is working on her 'certification' as a planner. In the process, she moved closer to home and is able to visit more often, taking advantage of the food and fellowship. With only the four youngest kids at home, we are a different family than she remembers. I actually think she likes coming home now!

Heidi is a junior at the University of Binghamton. She is a resident assistant (RA), which means she is the floor 'mother'. She has had her challenging moments, but her gentle spirit is having a soothing effect on the wild animals. Her major is Art. We have several of her 'inspired and inspiring' pieces displayed in the house. Perhaps I should start charging admission when people come to visit!

Well, the life of our family seems to have turned into one constant, crazy, glorious miracle. I'm glad I can't see into the future! I have a sense of anticipation that 1994 will NOT be boring!

May you bask in Love during this coming year!

With Peace and Joy,

Bob and Mary Young & Family

Christmas picture 1993.

This is a picture of Bob and Mary with Pope John Paul II taken in 1993.

Mary asked Pope John Paul II to bless our family. Wow!

Here is Pope John Paul II giving us our mission.

Here is a picture taken in August of 1994 of me with my 1976 yellow Mercedes the day I sold it for $200. It had carried me safely for 202,000 miles.

November 1995

Dear Friends,

Merry Christmas from the YOUNG's! Mary asked me to put together a note which brings you up to date since our last letter in December of 1993. We didn't succeed in getting a letter out last year.

Christie married Greg Sherwood in June! One year earlier, Greg, fortified by a *huge* diamond ring, popped the big question. They met four years ago when they both worked for Ciba-Geigy.

The wedding was *GREAT*! Mary was consumed for six months preparing. However, since she had one wedding under her belt, this one was easier. I created a little excitement the day before the wedding when, due to a car malfunction, I drove into the house going about thirty miles an hour. When Ryan saw the nearly totaled car protruding into the basement, he expressed best what everyone else was thinking, "What *idiot* did this?"

Christie and Greg are now living in Baltimore. They just announced that we will be grandparents in May of next year! I guess becoming a grandparent is God's way of giving a parent a promotion! *Grand* parent . . . it has a certain ring to it . . .

Angela and Tim are living in Binghamton. Angela spends most of her time engaged as a Catholic lay evangelist. She has a "talk" radio program called "The Catholic Connection". Tim continues working on his doctoral program in clinical psychology. I'm not sure what Tim is going to do for his doctoral thesis; but I notice that when he's around our family he's always observing and taking notes, murmuring aloud, "Wow . . . oohhhh . . . gosh . . . fascinating . . . ."

Nichole lives in Albany, and works as a financial planner. She helps other people manage their money . . . Scary, isn't it? Mary and I had been trying to get her more interested in church for several years. We finally gave up; but God came through! She found a church in the *mall*. Yes, this is America . . . *Mass* in the *mall*! I haven't questioned Nichole, but I'll bet during the collection, they ask, "Cash or charge?"

Heidi graduated Summa Cum Laude from the University of New York at Binghamton in June with a degree in Fine Arts. She is specializing in Christian art. She has held two very successful art shows: one in college last spring, and one this summer in Mt. Kisco. As a result of her shows, she made the front page of the Catholic New York newspaper, which in turn generated several jobs for her. Currently, she is doing eleven paintings for a nearby parish; they are going to put a "Heidi original" in each classroom of their new school. Heidi is currently living with us and functioning as our live-in spiritual guide, family therapist, baby-sitter, chauffeur, and maid . . . in other words, she is practicing motherhood.

Robert is attending Worcester State College in Massachusetts, where he transferred so he can study occupational therapy. He is known as "Reverend Rob" due to his continual effort to evangelize. As the recently elected President of the Newman Club, he's trying to develop a band of apostles to help spread the Word on campus.

Ryan graduated from high school in June, and is attending the Franciscan University at Steubenville, Ohio. He was awarded "Catholic Student Leader of the Year" by the pastor here for his pro-life activities his senior year. At Steubenville, he introduced himself to all the girls when he arrived, then all the new boys introduced themselves to him so that he could introduce them to the girls. Needless to say, he was elected freshman representative to the student government by an overwhelming landslide.

Marianne is sixteen, and a junior in High School. Her transition from child to young woman has been an interesting and exhausting experience for her, and those of us around her. It seems that God has chosen this point in time to bring to her tremendous suffering, and move her, and us, from spiritual childhood to sainthood. I'm going to petition the Pope to remove the Book of Job from the Bible, and replace it with the Book of Marianne! As she continues to struggle, she inspires all of us. On a lighter note, she just passed her driver's test, and now has her license. I recently heard her singing in the shower, "Free at last, free at last; thank God, free at last . . . "

Russell is in the eighth grade. I used to worry that my kids would grow long hair and become "hippies". No need to fret. Russell shaved his head. Also, he decided to become a policeman since "all they do is eat donuts." Speaking of food, Russ is into cooking; or, perhaps I should say, he's into eating . . . Mary found two spoons and a bowl of brownie batter in the cedar closet . . . .

Heather is in the sixth grade, her first year of "middle school". I asked her how she liked it. She said, "It's great, except for the academics!" She loves basketball, soccer, swimming, and art. I notice that when she speaks, she continually uses the word "whereas." Perhaps she's planning on becoming a lawyer.

Mary and I took a tour to the Holy Land this fall. It was delightful! My sister, Mary Jean, and her husband, Orrin, came with us on the tour, which made it even more special. Prior to that, in August, the entire family went on what has now become the "annual camping trip." To put this into perspective, I believe in spiritual terms our family is currently in the "purgative stage". This is when God gives you a spiritual check-up . . . rubber glove and all. Well, the family camping trip became our spiritual boot camp. "Roughing it" seems to magnify one's vices, and minimize one's virtues. It became apparent that I, for one, am attached to comfort. After a week of sleeping like a pretzel, constantly feuding with bees, and taking cold showers, my good humor was sorely tested. We went into the trip thinking we were the Partridge family; we came out realizing we were the Munsters. The highlight of the trip was the recitation of the Rosary under the stars. We realized, looking up at the numerous stars in the endless sky, that when we die, we get to meet the Person that created the Universe . . . awesome!

Well, to summarize, I'd say the Young family is entering a new phase. The highs are higher; the lows are lower. We are becoming more *conscious*. The spiritual roots are going deep in search of the Living Water. The Lord is giving us more opportunities to love and to serve, to listen and to suffer, to heal and to redeem. We are blessed!

May you experience in 1996 the Grace of God more fully!

With Peace, Joy, and Love,

Bob and Mary Young, & Family

<u>NEWS ALERT</u>: Angela just informed us that she is pregnant also! Due in July.

Christmas picture 1995.

Here is a picture of Bob and Mary after we renewed our wedding vows at Cana in the Holy Land.

The picture below shows Angela and Mary's dad, Paul Hoff, looking at the damage I did when I "drove" the Mercury car Paul sold to me through the open garage door and into the interior wall of our house.

December 1996

Dear Friends,

Merry Christmas from the YOUNGs! Mary asked me to summarize the annual happenings.

The highlight of the year was the three deliveries. Christie and Greg delivered Justin Michael in May. Angela and Tim delivered Zacchaeus Daniel in June. And Nichole delivered a twenty-nine pound Salmon in November. Mary is in ecstasy being a Grandmother. My excitement is tempered by the realization that the Young clan has two more mouths to feed. Nichole's fish took some pressure off. Perhaps next year she can deliver a twenty-nine pound loaf of bread . . . .

Heidi continues to live with us and create Christian art. One of her paintings was used for the front cover and centerfold of the Mother's Day issue of Our Sunday Visitor, a national Catholic newspaper. She is also teaching art part-time in the local schools for an after-school enrichment program. She bought her first car this year. It's a clunker. She's had only one accident so far. One of her jobs around the house is to vacuum. During Thanksgiving vacation, I heard the vacuum cleaner running continuously for over two hours. I was impressed that Heidi was taking her housework so seriously. I was surprised to discover that the sound was coming from a tape recording of a running vacuum cleaner. Angela uses the recording to lull Zacchaeus to sleep.

Robert is still attending Worcester State College in Massachusetts. He is majoring in occupational therapy. He's President of the Newman Club, a campus service organization. He's also teaching religion to high school students. Last summer he worked as a camp counselor and freelance baby-sitter. One of Rob's greatest virtues is perseverance. He's the only student in the history of Worcester State College that was successful in getting back his housing damage deposit. He overcame the bureaucracy with a six month letter-writing campaign, followed by a series of lengthy meetings with the Director of Housing. Now, when Rob enters the campus administration offices, one can hear a collective, audible groan from the staff.

Ryan is a sophomore at the Franciscan University at Steubenville, Ohio. His current plans are to pursue a career as a Physician's Assistant. He continues to be involved in the student government. Last year, he was a "senator". This year he's a "judge". He was picked up for speeding last summer and is going to court in December. So now, Judge Ryan will have an opportunity to meet the judge of the traffic court to explain why he was going twenty-six miles-an-hour over the speed limit. I've been trying to teach him how to fall to his knees and humbly beg for mercy. However, he still wants to engage in a logical debate with the magistrate. Why *is* it that God reserves the gift of Wisdom for parents?

Marianne is a senior in high school this year. She is very busy with her schoolwork, her after-school job, and her volunteer work. She was recently named to the academic honor society. She's the student executive in charge of coordinating the school support for the Battered Women's Shelter. She's currently grieving the loss of her favorite companion—the 1985 Honda that belonged to Christie, then to Nichole, and finally to me. The car had 174,000 miles on it. When someone offered me $800 for it, I sold it on the spot. I don't believe that selling "her" old car was a heartless, insensitive, mercenary act. Do you?

Russell is a freshman in high school. Mary and I are shocked at how hard he's studying this year. He's become a serious student, at least for the time being. I suspect it's fashionable for the girls to be attracted to the studious types. He has some good friends. One of them is here so often, we asked him if he wanted to be in our family Christmas picture. I'm hoping I can claim him as a dependent on my income tax. Russell is into gadgets. The basement has become a hospital for bikes. My lawn tractor has been modified to become a snow-plow. My leaf-rakes have been mysteriously replaced with mechanized blowers. There's a mini power blackout in the house when the light switch in his room is flipped on. Activated devices include a stereo, year-round Christmas lights, and a computer. We made a "loft" for his room. Basically, we built a four-foot platform for his mattress. The space underneath resembles a cave, and is his favorite place to hang-out. Russell is best described as a caveman with a shaved head living in the electronic age masquerading as a normal high school student.

Heather is in the seventh grade. Last summer she practically lived at the "club", where she played tennis, swam, and interacted with her friends. She continues to be a member of the traveling soccer team. Last month she made the traveling basketball team. Now, she's in Heaven! Last winter I coached her in basketball. It was a great bonding experience. She still likes me. She won't be a teenager until next July.

Mary and I are entering a new phase of our life. I have started the four-year formation program to become a Catholic Deacon. Mary attends classes with me two nights a week, and two Saturdays a month. The primary function of a Deacon, and his wife, is to be voluntary ministers of charity for the local parish community. At the conclusion of the program, I will receive the Sacrament of Holy Orders and will be authorized to give homilies and administer the Sacraments of Baptism and Holy Matrimony.

Mary is going through her change of life. She has two personalities lately. Her "old self" is a home-bound, dedicated, barefoot and pregnant mother that cleans, cooks, and caters to perfection. Her "new self" is an out-bound, independent Grandmother that creates, coordinates, connects, and contends. Needless to say, the change is causing the rest of the family to make some adjustments. Now I know how the plantation owners in the South felt after losing the Civil War.

I finished writing a book this year. It's a fictional novel about a middle-aged businessman that gets zapped by God and undergoes a major religious conversion. I currently plan on entitling it *Resurrected*. I agree; it's a far-out theme . . . but what the heck! It may never be published, but writing it was therapeutic. I've resisted Mary's advice to give the book to a therapist so that I can be psychoanalyzed. I'm *afraid* that if I were *healed* and became *sane*, I'd become a social outcast . . . like Jesus. Since I'm inclined to keep a low profile, I'm tempted to remain insane for a while longer.

Well, the Lord continues to bless our family. For that, we are thankful. Our desire is that you and your family will experience God more fully in 1997!

With Peace, Joy, and Love,

Bob and Mary Young, & Family

Christmas picture 1996.

December 1997

Dear Friends,

Merry Christmas from the YOUNGs! Mary asked me to write a short letter with the annual highlights.

This year there were no new grandchildren, no new children, and no weddings. Mary did not get on an internet chat room, find a friend, and abandon the family. I did not get fired, nor did I quit my job. We did not lose our entire retirement savings in the stock market. We did not run for political office. We were not voted "Parents of the Year." We did not sue anyone. We were not sued. None of our cars died, nor did we have any car accidents. We did not experience impotence. We did not visit the Pope. The house was not destroyed by fire nor by a fierce windstorm. We were not physically attacked by anyone. We were not publicly ridiculed, nor were we the object of slanderous rumors. We did not join a cult. We did not march in protest. We did not get hair transplants or boob jobs or face lifts, nor did we dye our hair. We did not run a marathon. We did not win the state lottery, nor did we buy a ticket. We were not exploited by the US Government, the New York State Government, the Westchester County Government, the New Castle Town Government, our Church, or our friends. To our knowledge, we were not the object of discrimination by any group or person based on our color, creed, sex, ethnic background, or sexual preference. We did not start nor participate in any international wars, nor any actions subversive to any political entities. We did not start smoking, nor did we start drinking more heavily. We did not start any fad diets, nor did we lose weight. Our phone bill has not gone down. We were not audited by the Internal Revenue Service. I did get, from IBM, a new, black laptop 133 mega-hertz computer with forty mega-bytes of memory, a two giga-byte hard drive and an 8X CD-ROM unit. *This was an incredible year!*

Next year might be even more interesting. Nichole and Ryan will be getting married (not to each other, thank goodness). Nichole will be getting married to Tim Quinn in Albany on May 30th. Ryan will be getting married to Elizabeth Robinson in Pittsburg on August 8th, prior to starting his last year of college. The grandsons, Justin and Zacchaeus, will celebrate their second birthdays in May and July respectively. Russell will get his driver's license. Heather (our baby!) will start High School. Heidi will do something unexpected. Rob will graduate from college. Marianne will start her second year of college. As for Mary and me . . . who knows? Perhaps some of the things that didn't happen to us this year will happen next year!

The family at home is dwindling. We are now a remnant. Also, due to the time Mary and I spend attending the Diaconate program, our habits are changing. The kids had a scare the other evening. They thought we had run out of Jeno's frozen pizza. Not to worry. I had fulfilled my fatherly duties and provided. Later that evening (true story), Russell's friend was complaining because their family had no frozen pizza. They had gone shopping and discovered that the local supermarket was sold out!

Heather continues to concern me. She's been a teenager since last July, and is still nice to me. She loves sports, particularly basketball and soccer—she's on the "traveling" teams. She's also into poetry. Her last poem was about a wolf attacking a chipmunk (I'm referring to animals; not sport teams).

Russell has become an entrepreneur. The other day I noticed in my back yard a neighbor kid doing Russell's leaf-raking. When questioned, the kid said Russell was paying him. Turns out, Russell is making so much money baby-sitting away from home that he decided to sub-contract his household chores. When I found out how much Russell was paying the kid, I asked if I could have the job next year!

Russ is looking for a new (girl) friend. To the last one that came, Mary said, "Oh, you must be *Wendy*! Russell has said so much about you." Turns out, this was a *new* girl and her name was *Jenny*.

Now Russell spends time with Michelle. He told Mary that Michelle beat him in arm wrestling. Mary said, "What! A girl beat you?" Russ countered, "Yeah. But she's the strongest girl in my grade."

Marianne is doing very well in her first year of college: good grades, good friends, and good attitude. Like her older brothers and sisters who left home to attend college, she now has an improved appreciation for her family and home life. She has chosen psychology as her college major. I think she wants to analyze herself. I'm okay with that. It sounds better than the local slander case where the defendant is a lawyer and plans to defend himself. It could get interesting when the lawyer cross-examines himself *under oath*. Based on existing trends, I'm sure someday soon some lawyer will divorce himself for infidelity to himself.

Ryan is training to be a Physician's Assistant—and is doing well. He spent a tough semester in Austria last spring taking German and other courses which will help him in his career. He must have an air of innocence about him. On three separate occasions he was robbed. Twice he lost credit cards that he didn't notice were missing. I wasn't too unhappy. The thieves were spending less money with the cards than Ryan.

Rob is going into "holistic medicine." No. He's not going to be a Priest. He's training to be an Occupational Therapist. His job is to help sick people work. There's a big market for this career field I'm told.

Heidi moved to Ohio for a few months to further develop her artistic talents, both on the canvas and in the kitchen. When her friends came to dinner, they stared at her painting of food until they salivated, then they ate the food she cooked. She found God in Ohio. The problem is that it's time now for her to come back to New York and I guess He doesn't want to leave Ohio.

Nichole is a business jet-setter during the week and a hunter and fisherwoman on weekends. Her fiancé, Tim, loves the outdoors. She joined the NRA, got a pick-up truck with a gun-rack, chews tobacco, and drinks Red Dog beer. (She's come a long way from the upper echelons of Sorority life.) Nichole is very adaptable.

Now that Angela and Christie have kids, they have a greater respect for their mother. But then, of course, Mary had *me* to help . . . . When Mary dies, they'll have to create a new category of Sainthood! Mary went to San Francisco for a wedding and was able to spend an afternoon sight-seeing with her family. They had a great time at the Costco Price Warehouse. Then that evening they all short-sheeted the beds of one another. It was an experience she will never forget.

As for me, I still work out of my home, in the basement, with my computer. I'm connected via E-mail to IBM, several of my kids, and some relatives. Occasionally I'm inconvenienced with a work-related message from someone in IBM. I told the kids that I was thinking about retirement. They seemed surprised to learn that I was still employed. Actually, I work a lot harder than they think, but I try to make it look easy . . . so they don't feel sorry for me . . . shut away in the basement . . . by myself . . . with the blinking screen . . . interacting . . . alone . . . (You can contact me at WWW. IAMLONELY.COM).

God bless you and your family!

With Peace, Joy, and Love,

Bob and Mary Young, & Family

Christmas picture 1997 taken in the Black Hills of South Dakota.

A picture of Bob and Mary on vacation in Aruba in 1997.

December 1998

Dear Friends,

Merry Christmas from the YOUNGs! Mary asked me to write a short letter with the annual highlights.

Nichole and Tim Quinn were married in Albany on May 30th. Ryan and Elizabeth Robinson were married in Pittsburgh on August 8th. Heidi and Peter Carucci became engaged and have plans to get married on July 3rd of next year.

Ryan is studying to become a Physician's Assistant. Earlier this year, he diagnosed Angela as having an enlarged pancreas. On November 1st, All Saints Day, her "enlarged pancreas" entered this world. They named it Maximilian Dominic. One nice thing about the names picked by Angela and Tim is that when they call the neighbors and ask them to send their kids home, it's unlikely the neighbor will ask "which Maximilian Dominic" and "which Zacchaeus Daniel?"

Christie and Greg are pregnant also. Justin's brother/sister is due next February. The Sherwood's live in North Carolina so we don't get to see them very often. Mary calls them, however. I felt sorry for her because she was getting a stiff neck from holding the portable phone to her ear with her shoulder as she worked. So I bought her earphones. Now she can talk "hands-free." It's a good thing for me that the phone rates have dropped to ten cents a minute. I figured it out. There are only 43,200 minutes in a month, so my maximum monthly phone bill is $4,320!

I went to North Dakota to visit my Mom in August. We had a real nice time. On the day before I was to leave to return to New York, she started to have a heart attack. She didn't want to disrupt my plans to go home, so she waited until after I left town to call 911 and go to the hospital. She's always been so thoughtful. She ended up having open heart surgery. Two months later, my ninety-year-old stepfather, Lloyd Bjella, died peacefully in her arms. They were married twenty-three years.

Russell turned sixteen last December. He got his driver's license this spring. He's only had two accidents so far. In both cases the accident could have been avoided if the people driving their cars in front of him hadn't stopped. In the first accident, my Mercury was totaled. In the second accident, my Nissan survived but there was $1,500 damage to the other car that was behind the school bus. Russell is very creative. Every few weeks he has a different hair color or style. I'm colorblind, but I think for Halloween he colored it red.

Heather turned fourteen in July. Last year I was worried because she became a teenager and was still nice to me. I'm not worried any longer. She started high school this year and is fully engaged in life. She's into tennis, soccer, basketball, swimming, music, friends, boys, Internet and academics. She is also very creative. She is a budding artist and a developing poet.

Marianne is in her second year of college at Binghamton University. She is still thinking of majoring in Psychology, or perhaps elementary education. She worked at a children's camp last summer and loved it. Last year she was a serious student. This year

I think she's shifted her focus to her social life. I'll be happy if she takes an accounting course so that she can learn how to balance a checkbook.

Rob is graduating from college this December with a degree in Occupational Therapy. He is currently living at home and doing his final field internship. He is applying for jobs in the area. His strategy is to mooch off his parents for a year while he gets established in a job and starts to pay off his college loans.

Heidi is also staying at home. In between making wedding plans, she is doing art, tutoring, doing volunteer work, developing housewife skills, making new friends, and meditating on the meaning of life.

Nichole is working her way up the corporate ladder. She works for a financial services company in Albany. She and her new spouse, Tim, are looking for a modern "cabin" with acreage so they can hunt deer in their backyard. I guess I understand. I have this desire to be a monk in a rustic hermitage on an isolated sandy beach on the Jersey shore.

Following their wedding in August, Ryan and Elizabeth drove cross-country to California for their honeymoon. They are living in Pittsburgh now as Ryan completes his fieldwork so that he can graduate in August as a Physician's Assistant. Elizabeth graduated in May with a degree in Biology. Ryan has already realized one of his biggest dreams in life: they have a 32-inch TV in their tiny apartment.

I am in my third year of the four-year program to become a Deacon in the Catholic Church. Mary attends most of the classes with me. It's like going back to college. As one of my social ministry projects I started doing bereavement counseling at the women's prison near here. Really—I did—I'm not kidding. It's been a very gratifying experience.

Mary and I enjoy going to movies to relax, although lately it is getting difficult to find a movie which promotes positive moral values. Recently we went to the local theater complex which has ten theaters. Mary looked up at the list of movies on the marquee and said, "I wonder what the movie 'All Positions' is about?" After studying the marquee, I responded, "I don't know what 'All Positions' is about. Nor do I know anything about the movie listed above it called 'Now Hiring'."

This is the year of the Bill Clinton scandal with the White House summer intern. I didn't have much sympathy for *him*, until Mary accused *me*. She said, "Bob, did you secretly eat *all* the ice cream I was saving for dessert?" I replied, "I never had intimate relations with the object in question. Although it is *possible* that the ice cream made contact with my body, I made no conscious, overt effort to respond. In fact, through mental telepathy I communicated to the ice cream that it was too early in our relationship for me to allow the act of eating to be consummated and that we should maintain a respectful distance." I continued responding to Mary in a firm voice filled with indignation, "Furthermore, I resent the obvious conspiracy by women to accuse men of secretly eating ice cream only to further their own politically inspired agenda—which is to control all men. Despite your accusations, there has been ice cream I have not eaten. Anyway, the kids say they are happy with me as a family provider, and want me to continue in that role without the distraction of your accusation. They want to know why you are not willing to put this to bed now that I have said that I once said I was sorry about something. And besides, what do you mean by the word '*all*?"

Keep smiling! It could be worse. Have a good year in 1999. God bless you and your family!

With Peace, Joy, and Love,

Bob and Mary Young, & Family

Christmas picture 1998.

This is a picture taken at Ryan and Elizabeth's wedding in 1998.

This is a picture taken at Nichole and Tim Quinn's wedding in 1998.

December 1999

Dear Friends,

Merry Christmas from the YOUNGs! Mary asked me to write a short letter with the annual highlights.

Last year Mary and I were experiencing the "empty nest" syndrome. There were only five people at home. It was somewhat depressing. However, the situation has changed. That feeling has disappeared. We now have eleven regular people in the house plus two people inside other people. I'll explain. Tim Lock is doing his internship for his Doctorate in Psychology at a nearby clinic. Tim, Angela, Zacchaeus, and Maximilian are now tenants. Angela is pregnant and due in April. Ryan and Elizabeth are also here as temporary tenants. Ryan graduated from college in August and is working as a Physician Assistant (PA) in New York City. Elizabeth graduated from college with a degree in Biology and is now attending school in the City to get her PA degree. She is pregnant and due in June. I'm not aware of any other woman in the house that is pregnant at this time.

Rob is living at home until next fall. He is engaged to Cara McEvoy, his longtime sweetheart. They are planning to be married in October. Rob has his degree in Occupational Therapy and is working full time at a nearby hospital. He moved out temporarily last summer to do an internship rotation. When he returned his room was taken, so we gave him a *closet* to live in—at a substantial discount in rent. Later he started use the adjacent hallway to store his stuff, so we raised his rent.

Events of each day frequently remind me of the current "full-nest" syndrome. The audio tapes in the car give clues as to whether the last driver was Angela, Russell, or Mary. The tapes range from "Baby Animals from Uncle Larry's Farm" to rap music called "Let's Blow up Something or Someone" to "Praise God from Whom All Blessings Flow." I play my personal meditation tape when I drive. I recorded it myself. It's the soothing sounds I hear in the morning when I'm reading my newspaper during my relaxation time—the sounds of a washer sloshing, a dryer spinning, the phone ringing, a child screaming. I call the tape "The Landlord Lullaby."

We have different users on the computer also. I'm never sure which program I might interrupt. It could be a game of electronic solitaire, an on-line chat with teenage boys, Reader Rabbit Preschool, or a regression analysis of the cognitive correlates of child abuse in adult survivors.

Katie Sherwood, our 4th grandchild, was born on February 1st. She lives in North Carolina with Greg, Christie, and Justin. Tim Quinn and Nichole bought a 60-acre "ranchette" near Albany. The entire family spent a long weekend camping out near a pond in their pasture. Neither Christie nor Nichole seems interested in moving home . . . yet.

Heidi and Peter decided to suspend their plan to get married this past July. They both wanted to spend some time pursuing other interests. Heidi moved out of the house and into an apartment. She started graduate school this fall and is working on her

Masters degree in Art. She is also planning to get her teaching credentials. In November she had a very successful solo art show.

Marianne is in her third year of college at Binghamton University. She is majoring in Psychology with a long term plan to teach elementary education. She's living off-campus this year. Now that she has to develop and manage a budget, she is getting quite good at writing e-mails to me with requests for additional funding. She often comes home on weekends to visit her favorite person—her three-year-old nephew, Zacchaeus. For a summer job she worked as a camp counselor for kids.

Russell is a senior in high school. He didn't have any car accidents this year. He has two jobs: during the week he baby-sits after school, and on weekends he works at a place called Party City (it's not what you think!). He teamed up with his friends and led the effort to build a two-story "house" in the woods near here. It's quite nice. It would be a great place for a homeless person. Russell turned 18 on December 6th and officially became an adult.

Heather is a sophomore in high school. She's very busy with her academics and sports. She made the varsity tennis team and the varsity basketball team. She also plays soccer on a traveling team.

Russell and Heather play in the band. Russell plays the tuba and Heather plays the saxophone. Heather wanted to cut band class one day because it was "so boring." Russell said, "I'm the one that should get permission to cut band. It's a lot more boring for me. I play only one-fourth as many notes as you!"

Mary and I have taught the kids how to be frugal and generous. This has created an unusual situation. Recently Rob returned home from the Methodist rummage sale and showed Mary the game he bought "at a great price." Mary laughed and said, "Rob, I donated that game to the sale. It used to be ours!" Angela bought a dress at the same sale. She discovered later that it once belonged to Heidi! So what's happening is this: the junk is moving within our house from one room to another via rummage sales, and the Methodists are making money on every transaction. I'm tempted to change religions.

Last summer I finished the first three years of the four-year Catholic Deacon program. I'm "on leave" from the program this year, although I'm continuing to stay involved in many of the activities, including my prison ministry. I'm not sure I'll be able to return to the program. They've added *sanity* as a prerequisite for ordination.

On the political scene, the Clinton's bought an older Colonial home in our town. Hillary is running for senator in New York and needed an instate residence. If I know Mary, she'll bring them a plate of cookies, welcome them, and say, "How many kids do *you* have?"

We're prepared for the Y2K apocalypse. Mary has stocked up on canned food, water, toilet paper, and cash. If the first thing we run out of is toilet paper, we'll have to make a difficult choice about the use of the cash. We had a rehearsal for the event in October—we were hit by Hurricane Floyd with a foot of rain. We spent five hours moving things out of the basement and bailing water. Turns out it was a great family bonding event. Ryan gave me a couple of aspirin so that I wouldn't have a heart attack. Thoughtful son!

The world is a safer place now that we *know* the tobacco companies sold us an *unhealthy product*. Can you *believe* they did this? Capitalist pigs! I'm thankful to the lawyers and public officials that uncovered this dirty little secret and administered justice with the half-a-trillion dollar lawsuit. I suspect that additional harm is being inflicted on us by the profit-hungry, multinational, faceless, amoral conglomerates that ply us with sugar, fatty meats, alcohol, and perverted movies. The time has come—the national mood is right—it's the American way: let's *sue* our way to health!

According to the messages given to the Visionaries at Fatima, God allowed Satan to have extended power during the Twentieth Century. It gives one hope that the first century of the next millennium will experience a reversal of this trend. I hope all of us can participate in the come-from-behind victory!

With Peace, Joy, and Love,

Bob and Mary Young, & Family

Christmas picture 1999.

December 2000

Dear Friends,

Merry Christmas from the YOUNGs! Mary asked me to write a short letter with the annual highlights.

Mary's dad, Paul Hoff, died in November at the age of 87. His peaceful death provided his family with an opportunity for unity and intimacy. They joined with him in praying the Rosary as he made the transition into the next life. His legacy includes 8 children, 27 grandchildren, and 18 great-grandchildren.

This year several people migrated out of the house. Those remaining in the house and renting space include Angela and Tim Lock, as well as Zacchaeus (4) and Maximilian (2). Tim graduated with his Doctorate in Psychology and is working full time for a mental health organization. Tim and Angela celebrated by co-creating a new eternal soul called Kateri Mary (born April 16). Also remaining in the house are Mary, myself, and Heather (16). Those who left this year include Rob, Ryan, Elizabeth, Marianne, and Russell.

Ryan and Elizabeth, along with their giant-sized TV, moved to New York City for a few months, and then settled in a small town near Poughkeepsie, about 50 miles north of us. Ryan is working for an ear/nose/throat surgeon as a Physician Assistant. Elizabeth is doing her internship and will also become a Physician Assistant. Their love has been incarnated and they call him Christopher Owen (born July 6).

Rob moved in with Cara McEvoy—after their wedding, of course. They were married in October. Following their two week honeymoon in Hawaii, they moved into an apartment in Greenwich Connecticut. They both commute thirty minutes to New York State where they work as occupational therapists. Cara knew that Rob was paying rent while living at home. However, I had never explained to her that most of the "rent" was for board. After living with him for a week, Cara timidly observed, "Gee, Rob, you sure eat a lot!"

Marianne completed her junior year in college. This summer she received a free trip to Rome to attend the Jubilee Youth Conference with Pope John Paul II. When she returned, she went on a four week spiritual retreat at a nearby hermitage. This year she is attending school part-time and works at a nearby parish as a secretary and bookkeeper. She's driving a car that was given to her as a gift. She's following the example of Heidi and trying to grow in the virtue of poverty.

Russell graduated from high school in May. He and I are being sued for 1.25 million dollars for his fender-bender car accident two years ago. The other driver is suing for 1.0 million and claiming "back injuries." His wife is suing for.25 million and claiming the "loss of services" of her husband. Wow! I had no idea of the value of a husband's "services." I'm renegotiating my contract with Mary. Over the summer Russ continued to work at a place called Party City. This fall we transported him, his stereo with gigantic speakers, his 2.3 gigahertz telephone, several cartons of cigarettes, his computer, and a few items of clothing to the State University of New York at Oneonta where he registered as a freshman. He has a major addiction. He's a spendaholic. In an attempt to help him cut back on his expenses, I agreed to buy discounted cigarettes for him using the Internet. After going to DirtCheapCigs.com and completing the transaction, I felt an overwhelming urge to take a shower and go to confession. Russell is majoring in accounting.

After living three years in North Carolina, Christie and Greg Sherwood moved back to Baltimore. Greg received a job promotion. They have two children: Justin (4) and Katie (2). Justin has a quick wit and a good sense of humor. A stranger asked him, "What does your dad do?" Without hesitating, my grandson responded, "He farts and poops his pants a lot." The stranger asked no more questions.

Nichole and Tim Quinn continue to live on their ranchette near Albany. Nichole works in the financial services area and, following a company merger, has greatly expanded responsibilities. She enjoys her work tremendously. Tim works as a biologist. They both love the outdoors and now have horses. Nichole drives her horse like a car—she doesn't know how to use the brakes. As a result, she fell off and broke her shoulder blade, but has since recovered. She has also expanded her interests into other areas. To the surprise of no one, she is teaching a Confirmation class this year . . .

Heidi is attending school full-time and plans to get a Masters degree in Fine Arts. She moved from Pleasantville to Yonkers and lives with two other young women. Like Marianne, she also received a free trip to Rome this year and, like Marianne, is also driving a car that was given to her as a gift. While in Rome, she was able to experience the fabulous art and architecture displayed in and around the Vatican. She supports herself by selling art and by working part time as a tutor and substitute teacher.

Heather lives at home and is the last of my children to get a driver's license. She is a junior in high school and turned sixteen this summer. Despite my extensive experience teaching the other kids how to drive, I get stressed when she is parallel parking in a small space and accidentally pushes the gas pedal rather than the brake. Last night she said proudly, "I've gone a whole week without having a near-accident!" She still loves sports, but has expanded her disciplined lifestyle to include her academics. She's a serious student and gets very good grades. For a summer job she worked as a receptionist at a nearby swim and tennis club. Also, I suspect she has a secret business arrangement with the local Mall. She brings home clothes, leaves them in her room for a month or two, returns them, and then brings home other clothes. I assume she has rented out her room to the Mall for temporary storage.

Many of you that have read my Christmas letters over the years have suggested that I write a book. Well, believe it or not, it's done! The title is *Calling All POWs.* It's a "fascinating" story about spiritual warfare. Angela was my chief proofreader. Heidi created a painting for the cover. It can be ordered online by using the bookstore at www. iUniverse.com. Phone orders can be placed by calling 1-877-823-9235 or by contacting your local bookstore. The ISBN number is 0-595-14897-2.

This was the first year that a movie theater gave Mary and me the "senior citizen" discount. I thought it was great. Mary said, "We have to tell them they made a mistake." I said, "No, it wouldn't be fair to embarrass the ticket person. And besides, perhaps we can take the extra six dollars and use it for a down payment on a box of popcorn." We got the entire family involved in the debate, and eventually voted to resolve the conflicting opinions. The vote is being contested now because we had one absentee ballot without a postmark, one ballot with a hanging chad, one ballot that was partly chewed by a small child, and one ballot with a dimpled chad. Furthermore, when we went to find a lawyer to help us resolve the conflict, we couldn't find one. They were all in Florida working to resolve the presidential election! After some discussion, Mary and I evaluated the current practice used by the US military and agreed on a "don't ask—don't tell" policy: I *won't tell* her what I paid for the tickets; and she *won't ask*.

May God bless you and your family in 2001!

With Peace, Joy, and Love,

Bob and Mary Young, & Family

Christmas picture 2000.

December 2001

Dear Friends,

Merry Christmas from the YOUNGs! Mary asked me to write a short letter with the annual highlights. Sorry that there is no picture this year. We were overwhelmed by the logistics.

Mary and I are beginning to experience the "empty nest syndrome." Angela and Tim bought a house 30 miles away in Brookfield, Connecticut and moved in November. Our grandchildren moved with them: Zacchaeus (5), Maximilian (3), Kateri (1.5), and?. Yes—the "?" means that Angela is pregnant! She is due early next summer. The house is really quiet. I already miss Kateri "Parasite" Lock begging me for part of my breakfast.

The move out by Angela and Tim was the first phase of our "archeological dig." Now we are negotiating with the other kids to convince them to remove their layers of stored treasures. Mary and I expect to find our stuff on the bottom of the excavation, if it hasn't turned into coal. We need to find the bottom because Mary and I are planning to sell the house next spring. Our "baby", Heather, starts college in September. Thus, Mary and I want to move into something different in preparation for our "golden years." We are struggling to develop a vision of our next house. We are debating between two alternatives: a small affordable, maintainable cottage; and a hotel-like mansion that will accommodate visits from our kids with their families.

Heather is enjoying her senior year of high school. She is graduating with honors and is feverishly investigating colleges. She is co-captain of her traveling soccer team. To earn money for college, she worked last summer as a receptionist at the local swim club. She is also baby-sitting on a regular basis. She hasn't had any car accidents . . . yet. Despite my "don't speed" directive, she did have a lapse and got a ticket. The state trooper said she was going 81 mph in a 55 mph zone. Turns out it was my fault. She explained to me that the map I had given her was confusing and she became lost . . . and that's why she was speeding. I knew better than to argue with that logic—I have six daughters and a wife.

Russell is a sophomore in college at the State University of New York at Oneonta. He survived his freshman year—not that Mary and I had any doubts . . . In fact, he succeeded to the extent that he was invited to be an RA (resident assistant). Apparently his studious behavior and disciplined demeanor impressed the people in charge of selecting the floor leaders. As an RA he has his own room—with adequate space for his computer, his TV, his VCR, his refrigerator, and a *tiny shelf* for books. This past summer Russ worked for the Town of Bedford maintaining and repairing roads. He had to be at work by 7 AM. His job provided him with the opportunity to experience a summer sunrise.

Marianne is working as a behavior specialist at a school for autistic children. She is taking college classes at night. She expects to graduate this spring with a degree in psychology. Her work is ideal for her—part teacher and part psychologist. She finds the job extremely demanding, but fulfilling. Her junker gift car is with us no more. The car had a bad habit of stalling. One day it stalled on the Whitestone Bridge in heavy traffic. There might be a worse place in the world to stall—but for now I can't think of one. I suggested that she have her car repaired at the local "bargain repair shop." Unfortunately the car died on the operating table. They worked on the car until it didn't run at all. To extricate ourselves from the situation, we just signed over the title to the garage. Then I convinced Marianne that she should buy a *new* car. She said, "Dad, you're crazy! I don't have any money." I said, "Marianne, this is America! You don't need *money* to buy something. This is the promised land: the land of milk and *credit*." Marianne is now driving a beautiful new Honda.

Ryan, Elizabeth, Christopher (1.5), and? are living in Poughkeepsie, New York, about 50 miles North.

Yes, you guessed it! The "?" means that they are "with child." March is the due date. Elizabeth received her certification as a PA (Physician's Assistant) in October. She is now working as a Radiology PA. Ryan continues to work as a PA also with an ear/nose/throat specialty. Like Marianne, they have also been enlightened. They bought a house with no money down. Life is great!

Christie, Greg, Justin (5), and Katie (3) continue to live near Baltimore, Maryland. Justin called me on my birthday. I was on my ladder washing the second-floor windows. Mary handed me the phone through an open window. Justin said, "Grandpa, happy birthday!" He paused, and then said, "How old are you?" Hanging on to the ladder precariously with one hand, and the phone with the other, I replied, "Fifty-eight." He said incredulously, "Fifty-eight! That's really old! . . . You should be dead!" Thanks to my ever-vigilant guardian angel, I managed to hang on to the ladder as I convulsed with laughter.

Nichole and Tim continue to live on their ranchette near Albany with their three horses and two cats. Nichole is a Vice President for a financial services firm and Tim works as a scientist. They hosted the family outing again this summer. This year Nichole talked Tim into joining her to help teach the Confirmation class. Nichole was intending to retire from that job but the kids convinced her to return.

Heidi is planning to graduate this spring with a Masters Degree in Fine Arts. She continues to share an apartment with two other young women in Yonkers. She paints extensively and earns enough to survive by selling her paintings and tutoring. Her junker gift car is still functioning. I believe there is a logical explanation. I believe there is a quote from Jesus in Scripture, "If you have *faith* the size of a mustard seed, you can actually *drive* a collection of loosely connected, worn-out car parts."

Rob and Cara live in Greenwich, Connecticut. They both are working as OT's (Occupational Therapists). A year of married life has passed, and they are still on their honeymoon . . . . Cara seems relaxed and happy. Rob thinks he has died and gone to heaven. They live a very active lifestyle. Cara is into art and dancing. Rob loves to ride his mountain bike. Rob tends to view life as a series of gourmet meals separated by short digestion periods. This perspective resulted in an awkward moment recently. He and Cara were entertaining their friends and he mistakenly assumed their wedding gift of engraved glass candlesticks were champagne glasses!

Mary continues to concern herself with the health of our family. For example, she ensures that we always have All-Bran cereal available. Well, I won't say that we eat too much All-Bran . . . but I'm happy to report that we have saved enough coupons from the boxes to earn a free airline ticket!

My book *Calling All POWs* has been wildly successful—most of my kids have read it. It can now be ordered from any bookstore. I also have a website at www.calltobefree. com with an "Ann Landers type" advice column for Spiritual Warfare POWs (i.e. those of us who go through life as prisoners of fear). I expect that as the cosmic war between supernatural good and supernatural evil intensifies and becomes more visible—ala the WTC Tragedy of September 11th and aftermath—the need will rapidly develop for supernatural anti-terrorist training. I anticipate that my next book will encompass what might be called "Boot Camp" for spiritual and emotional prisoners of war.

We look forward to hearing from you. May God bless you and your family in 2002!

With Peace, Joy, and Love,

Bob and Mary Young, & Family

Christmas picture 2001.

A picture of Bob and Mary taken in 2001.

December 2002

Dear Friends,

Merry Christmas from the YOUNGs! Mary asked me to write a short letter with the annual highlights. Thanks to technology there is a "family" picture this year. We transitioned to an 8x10 collage.

We have moved to Danbury Connecticut! We downsized, but still have enough room for Russell and Heather over the summer break from school. During the school year it's just Mary and me at home . . . . Whew!

After living in our large house in NY for 24 years, moving was no small challenge. Mary and I were initially tempted to keep a lot of junk. Fortunately, however, our moving capacity changed at the last minute. As I was driving one of the rented moving trucks to pick up our stuff, I drove under a very low bridge and instantly converted the large moving van into a flatbed truck. My accomplishment was not without distinction. The investigating cop said, "You're the first person to hit that bridge and make it all the way through!"

Heather is a college freshman and is attending the nursing program at Binghamton University in NY. The process of selecting her school and major was agonizing, but we are all comfortable with her final decision. Ultimately she'd like to become a Nurse Practitioner. She had a great senior year in high school: graduated with honors; played soccer; wonderful prom; great summer job at the pool; loads of nice friends. She also loves college. At college they have an intramural boy/girl football team and the boys elected her quarterback. She seems convinced that she has died and gone to heaven! She had full use of a car this summer and only had three fender-bending encounters.

Russell is in his third year of college at the State University of NY at Oneonta. He loves being an RA (resident assistant). He's majoring in accounting. At the end of last semester he became very upset and confused when he got a letter indicating that he was on the "Dean's List." He was visibly relieved when I explained that the Dean's List is a *good thing*—it's the academic honor roll. This summer he worked as a bank teller. After a couple of days on the job, I asked, "How do you like the work?" He said, "It's a little boring." I said, "So, you'd rather blacktop roads again—like last summer?" He smiled and said, "No. I *love* being a bank teller." He used a portion of his summer earnings to reward himself with a new computer. He needed a bigger hard disk to store the movies he was downloading from the Internet.

Marianne graduated with honors from Binghamton University with a degree in Psychology. She is working full-time in a school for autistic kids. The work is demanding, but fulfilling. She recently received a big promotion from behavior specialist to teacher. In the evenings she attends graduate school. She has started work on her Master's Degree. For excitement she attended the World Youth Day in Toronto this year with her good friends and the Pope. One of her favorite activities is to spend time with her nieces and nephews.

This has been a major transitional year for Heidi. She earned her Master's Degree in Fine Arts, was commissioned to paint some murals, bought a new car, worked as the Assistant Director of a summer Youth Camp, traveled to Australia, obtained a full time position teaching art at Archbishop Stepinac (all boys) High School in White Plains, became engaged to Nicholas Paris, and got a cell phone.

We have two new grandchildren this year. Trinity Marie Young joined this world in Poughkeepsie NY on March 12th. She lives with Ryan, Elizabeth, and Christopher (2). Ryan and Elizabeth are both working as Physician Assistants. Therese Mary Lock arrived in Brookfield CT on June 13th. She lives with Tim, Angela, Zacchaeus (6), Maximilian (4), and Kateri (2). Tim is a psychologist and this year started his own practice. Angela is attempting to get more organized. She may be getting *too zealous*, however. Therese Marie was still in the womb when the planned date of her Baptism ceremony arrived.

Christie, Greg, Justin (6), and Katie (4) continue to live near Baltimore MD. Greg is the Director of Materials Management for Alpharma (a pharmaceutical company). Christie and the kids came up and helped us unpack after the move to the new house. During the same trip she volunteered to paint Angela's kitchen. Heidi completed the project with a mural of flowers.

Nichole and Tim Quinn have progressed further into their "farming" adventure. They bought some chickens. Nichole has been trying to "housebreak" them. They sit on her lap when she watches TV. However, until she succeeds in getting them completely housebroken, Mary and I will likely continue to limit our visits. Of the things I like to do, watching TV with a chicken on my lap is not one of them.

Rob and Cara continue to work as Occupational Therapists. They bought a house in Danbury CT. They have been spending time personalizing the property. Their last improvement was an 18-foot wooden bridge over a creek that runs through their yard. Rob is the first of our children to own a bridge. Mary and I are quite proud.

Mary has been working diligently trying to furnish our "new" home in Danbury. At first she seemed to be psychologically immobilized by the fearful idea of spending substantial amounts of money for furniture. However, based on her recent glut of purchases, there is evidence of a miraculous healing.

Our "new" four-bedroom colonial home is actually two years old. Both the house and the yard are low-maintenance. A lawn service cuts my grass every week. My air-conditioned office is on the second floor and has two windows. I have cable TV for the first time in my life. I have a cell phone and a car, and so does Mary. I have a spare car for the kids. I have a high speed DSL link for my computer. Every morning my loving wife makes me a perfect fried egg, a toasted bagel, a homemade bran muffin, and a large glass of orange juice with lots of pulp. I am regularly allowed to consume large dishes of fat-filled Haagen Dazs ice cream. And finally, our Master bedroom is nice and large with an area for reading and with a spa-sized bathtub—our bedroom is

Christmas picture 2002.

Bob and Mary

Russ, Marianne

Heather

Christie, Greg,
Justin, Katie

Ryan, Elizabeth
Christopher, Trinity

Heidi, Nicholas

Tim and Nichole

Rob and Cara

< Angela, Tim, Zacchaeus,
Therese, Maximilian, Kateri

Here is a picture of me with the moving truck I was driving. In the background you can see the low bridge that I went under . . . sort of.

This is a picture of our new home in Danbury, Connecticut.

December 2003

Dear Friends,

Merry Christmas from the YOUNGs! As you can see from the "wide-angle" family picture this year, we are still experimenting with technology. Our photo depicts the major family event of the year: the wedding of Heidi to Nicholas Paris. Nicholas became family member number twenty-five. As you might notice from the picture template, family member number twenty-six was in the picture also . . . hiding in the womb of Cara. Yes! Rob and Cara are expecting their first child in early February!

My 36 year marathon working for IBM is complete! I retired in October shortly after my 60th birthday. Mary and I celebrated by making a pilgrimage to Medjugorje to initiate the post-IBM phase of our lives.

Mary actually has an official job outside the home. She is functioning as the Vice President of Operations for our son-in-law, Dr. Tim Lock. He taught her how to use the computer to run the business side of his practice. Our kids were somewhat shocked when they discovered their mom sending e-mails to them—actually multiple duplicate e-mails because, when the computer didn't react quickly enough, she hit the "send" button several times. Her knowledge goes far beyond the mere sending of e-mail. Heather called her one day to ask her how to get some gum out of her clothes. Mary explained, "Well, sign onto the Internet, find the website for Heloise using the search engine called Google, and then look up Gum." Heather was speechless.

Russell added a third computer to his inventory. He decided he needed a laptop at college to use during class to take notes. He said he couldn't read his own handwriting and was afraid his grades might suffer. I decided it was easier to let him buy another computer than to convince him to improve his handwriting. Also, as a side benefit, he is now enabled during class to send me an instantaneous request for more money. He is currently scheduled to graduate in December of 2004 with a degree in accounting.

Heather is a sophomore in college and is continuing to follow the Nursing curriculum and to acquire caregiver skills. She especially loves her class in kickboxing. Mary and I visited her college in November and watched her play soccer and football. After observing her quarterback the intramural mixed boy/girl football team to a 65-14 victory I asked, "Don't people get discouraged playing against your team?" She said, "Not really. They don't expect to do any better." I'm not sure she really minds the rumor going around that some students refer to her as the "football goddess."

Marianne continues to teach at Devereaux, a nonprofit institution that works with autistic kids. It is grueling work, but fulfilling for her. She is on the fast-path to sainthood. At night she takes classes towards her Master's Degree in Special Education. She has a great group of close friends. She recently discovered that the large white object in her kitchen is called a "stove" and that it can be used to cook food. Sell your stock in Dunkin Donuts!

Nichole and Tim hosted a fall festival for the family. They created a miniature Disneyworld in their pasture. They had a huge jumping gym, hay rides, apple-bobbing, face painting, fishing, horse rides, and of course, lots of food. Nichole continues to break bones in her body. First there was the skiing accident. She broke her collarbone. Then she was on the losing side of an encounter with one of her horses. She scolded the horse and hurt his feelings. He turned around, backed up, kicked her, and broke her arm. Despite her handicaps, she flies about the country for her job at Bank of America—asking strangers, "Could you please help me with my bags?"

Christie, Greg, Justin (7), and Katie (5) continue to live in Baltimore. During a recent stay with us, Katie and I were sitting alone at the breakfast table. I was moved by the Spirit and began to sing. Katie turned to me, smiled, and said sweetly, "Grandpa, let's play the quiet game."

Angela, Tim, Zacchaeus (7), Maximilian (5), Kateri (3), and Therese (1) live 10 miles away in Brookfield. When we want to remember what it was like raising our kids, we visit them. My memory returns more quickly than Mary's. Prior to taking a plane trip over the Pacific, Tim studiously showed Maximilian a map of the Pacific Ocean. Then, as they flew over the ocean, Maximilian peered out the window and fixed his gaze on the water below. When asked why, he answered, "I'm looking for the letters."

Heidi and Nicholas are adjusting well to married life. Heidi cooked her first big dinner for her mother-in-law: a Thanksgiving turkey. It was a near-perfect evening. I'm sure she isn't the first person to leave the bag of loose parts inside the turkey she cooked.

Rob and Cara decided to take a giant step forward on the road to enlightenment. Their first baby is due in February. Cara has experienced every form of morning sickness but seems to be managing the constant discomfort. When the tiny bundle of Joy arrives, Rob can be a more active participant in the care-giving team. In preparation, he had major surgery to remove significant portions of his throat (to resolve a sleep apnea condition). He now requires less sleep.

Ryan, Elizabeth, Christopher (3), and Trinity (1) are still living in Poughkeepsie. Elizabeth had some unplanned plastic surgery on her nose. She and Ryan were in a car accident while away on vacation. She now has a nose that is the envy of the entire Young family. Ryan had a near-death experience. He had an allergic reaction to some sinus medicine. He was able to diagnose himself and have Russell drive him to the emergency room. Fortunately for Russell they got there in time to apply an antidote. That way Russell didn't have to watch Ryan give himself an emergency tracheotomy in the car.

Retirement is wonderful. Imagine waking up every morning and it is Saturday! The only scary part is that I feel like I'm on a spaceship with only enough fuel (money) to last a finite amount of time. I guess the idea is to run out of breath before you run out of money. Ha! Anyway, Jesus says in the Bible, "Look at the birds in the sky, they gather nothing into barns, yet your heavenly Father feeds them. Do not worry. Seek first the kingdom of God and everything else will be given to you besides." Well, of course I have faith in that promise, but I'm not going to destroy my credit cards until I get a personal, direct and unequivocal command from the Big Guy! If that command does come, you'll probably see me donning a yellow "Big Bird" suit and hop around looking like I don't have a care in the world. If things fail to develop as I anticipate, perhaps some state institution will provide me with room, board, and a white coat.

This is the time of the year to count one's blessings. I'm no exception. My lovely wife has managed to help me get this far—thank you God! My kids keep me connected to Reality. My grandkids are conduits of Joy and innocent Love. I'm a rich man!

We look forward to hearing from you. May God bless you and your family in 2004! With Peace, Joy, and Love, Bob and Mary Young, & Family

Christmas picture 2003.

This is a picture of Bob and Mary in 2003.

December 2004

Dear Friends,

Merry Christmas from the YOUNGs!

Our family continues to grow. In January, Emma Elizabeth Young arrived. Rob and Cara are the proud parents. It's their first time. In November, Miguel Joseph Lock arrived. Tim and Angela were responsible for his entry into this world. Miguel is their fifth. He was preceded by Zacchaeus, Maximilian, Kateri, and Therese. We now have twenty-seven people in our extended family. As for me, I feel like Abraham. I can see it coming. "Your descendents will be as numerous as the stars in the sky!"

Heather is in her third year of college working on her degree in nursing. Last month she started the transition from theory to practice. It was quite a shock for her when, for the first time, she had to give a bath to another adult (an older gentleman). She is definitely growing in wisdom and virtue! She is living off campus in an apartment this year with several of her friends and is enjoying it immensely.

This was a big year for Russell. This month he graduated from college with a degree in Accounting. All in all, his achievement can now be classified as an official miracle. His peak of rebellion occurred in high school, which allowed him to settle into college earlier than most of his peers. The entire family is proud of his success . . . and pleasantly surprised. Fortunately, before returning to school for his last semester, he totaled the car that he was using, so he didn't have to deal with that distraction. Last summer he had an opportunity to practice working in the real world of business. Each day he commuted two hours into New York City to work as an intern for the Bank of America . . . and he survived!

Marianne moved to Danbury this past year. At first we thought it was because several other family members are living in and around this area, but then we realized that this is the epicenter for Dunkin Donuts! There are seven outlets here. In conjunction with her move, she tried to donate her extra furniture to the Salvation Army. They rejected her offer. I guess they didn't want to embarrass the poor people by asking them to take her stuff.

Mary and I have told our kids repeatedly, "Don't ever get a dog, it's too much work." The kids have always accepted that advice, until this year. Ryan and Elizabeth broke free from our parental guidance and added a puppy to their family. Christopher and Trinity were delighted. Everyone was happy . . . for the first few hours. Mary checked in with them a week later. Ryan explained that, in one week, the puppy had trashed the house. You really can't blame the puppy. He didn't know the difference between a toilet and a house. They gave the puppy away, but still have a pet. Christopher found a mouse in the house and was playing hide and seek with it. He couldn't understand why his mom and dad jumped screaming onto a kitchen chair.

Nichole and Tim hosted the family outing again this year. When I retired last fall, my kids gave me money for a digital camera. So I used the occasion of the camping trip to snap 250 random pictures of the family swimming, eating, playing, eating, riding, eating, laughing, and eating. Then I put the pictures to music and produced a DVD to memorialize the family communion showing the communal commingling and culinary consumption.

Katie Sherwood started kindergarten this year. Justin is in the third grade. Christie and Greg are adjusting quite well to the "empty nest syndrome."

When Angela was seven months pregnant with Miguel, Maximilian, age 5, asked, "How does that baby get out of your womb?" Angela replied, "It's a lot of work." Maximilian mused, "It must be kind of tricky!"

Now that Emma is nearly a year old, Rob and Cara decided to prepare for her future. They bought a larger home in an adjacent town called Ridgefield. This decision gave Nick and Heidi the opportunity to buy Rob and Cara's home in Danbury.

Nick and Heidi seem to be enjoying immensely their first year of married life. Nick is very sensitive to Heidi's needs. When she complained that her feather pillow was too thick, he decided to surprise her and solve the problem. He cut the pillow open to take out some of the feathers. The result was unexpected. Now, like Nichole, they have a home that contains floating fluff from friendly fowl.

I've been retired for a year now. It's *more* than it's cracked up to be! Having *no commitments* can be very addicting. I'm committed to continuing this regimen of non-commitment. Mary and I continue to grow closer as each day passes. We understand and accept one another better now that our kids have diagnosed me as "autistic" and her as "ADD." For those who are unfamiliar with these terms, that means that I am very attached to my schedule and routines, and get quite agitated when there is any change. In Mary's case, the kids say that she has attention deficit disorder (ADD). We always knew she could do *five* things at once. What we never understood is that she can't do *one* thing at once. Live and learn! Good thing the kids have some medical knowledge.

We look forward to hearing from you. May God bless you and your family in 2005!

With Peace, Joy, and Love,

Bob and Mary Young, & Family

Christmas picture 2004.

Tim and Nichole Quinn

Heidi and Nicholas Paris

The Sherwoods: Christie, Justin, Katie, Greg

Bob and Mary

The Locks:
Maximilian, Kateri, Angela, Miguel, Tim, Therese, Zacchaeus

Christopher, Ryan, Trinity, Elizabeth   Cara, Emma, Rob   Marianne, Russell, Heather

December 2005

Dear Friends,

Merry Christmas from the YOUNGs! Mary asked me to write a short letter with the annual highlights.

This was a growth year for the family. Our inventory of grandchildren grew by 30 percent bringing the total to thirteen. October was the banner month. James Robert Young was born on October 6th and joined Rob, Cara, and Emma. Two days later Grace Elizabeth Young joined Ryan, Elizabeth, Christopher, and Trinity. Two days passed and then Nicholas Joseph Paris arrived underwater in a birthing center. His parents are Heidi and Nicholas. Grandma (Mary) experienced a grandchild overdose condition: she had trouble knowing how to allocate her time to meet the needs of all the exhausted mothers while continuing to serve her needy husband (me!) in her traditional outstanding manner. But, of course, she managed to pull it off with aplomb. All the babies are healthy and happy. During Heidi's labor the midwife sent Nicholas to get some Caster Oil to speed up the contractions. Not having heard of the term "Caster Oil", Nicholas went to the nearest supermarket and asked a checkout person for help. Thankfully, on his way out of the store with a quart of Castrol motor oil, he was inspired by Heidi's guardian angel to verify his selection with the pharmacist.

All the excitement of the babies did, however, cause some family processes to be stressed beyond their design capacity. The first incident that came to my attention was the existence of *two* open boxes of my General Mills brand of Corn Chex cereal. This should never happen. But, like a good Catholic, I decided that this situation, like the Trinity and the Incarnation, was an unexplainable mystery. Then about two weeks later I was shocked to notice there were now *three* open boxes of my cereal. Mary was in the kitchen with me, so I turned and said, "How is it possible that there are *three* open boxes of Corn Chex?" Her face went through a series of contortions. Finally she spoke. "Have you noticed that these Corn Chex taste any differently?" I responded naively to my trustworthy wife of 39 years, "Why are you asking me that question?" She went on to say, "Well, for the past three months I have been buying boxes of the cheap no-name brand of Corn Chex and using them to fill your empty General Mills Corn Chex boxes. I save $2.50 a box that way." Needless to say I was amazed with the depth of planning required to successfully execute the deception. I didn't know whether to call the SEC or a priest to deal with this corporate scandal. Anyway, we have moved on. I have forgiven her and have acquiesced. I now eat the substandard cereal. Hopefully the long-term psychological impact on me will be manageable. My doctor told me on a recent visit that I could live another 20 years. I only need 16, so I plan to sell 4 on eBay. The other night I was settled in with my customary large dish of ice cream and was contemplating which 4 years to sell, when I noticed that the "vanilla zing" in my Haagen Dazs was missing. My mind started racing . . . I felt faint . . . my frugal wife wouldn't be at it again . . . or would she?

The remainder of the family reaped the benefits of Mary's frugality also. When the next door neighbor moved he cleaned out his house and filled a dumpster in his driveway. Late one night Mary and Nichole raided the dumpster and found, among other things, some unopened cans of chili. Our unaware family seemed to enjoy the free meal provided by Divine Providence and the two scavengers.

Both Heather and Marianne had an opportunity to make a pilgrimage to the town of Medjugorje in Europe this year. Both had life-changing experiences. They went at different times with different groups. Heather went over with a group led by the Franciscan Friars of the Renewal. Marianne went with a group that stayed in the home of one of the Visionaries. Heather plans to graduate next May with a degree in Nursing. Marianne will be getting her Master's degree in Special Education.

Russell is still working for Bank of America. Early this year Nichole was promoted within Bank of America and now commutes during the week from Albany NY to Boston MA rather than to New York City. Russell was promoted in September and moved from New York City to Boston. He and Nichole share an apartment. Nichole and her husband, Tim, still enjoy immensely their ranchette in Albany. Tim thrives on hunting, fishing, and golfing. Nichole continues to have a special relationship with her chickens and horses. She broke a bone again during her annual ski vacation. She is on a first name basis with her orthopedic surgeon.

Christie, Greg, Justin, and Katie are still in Baltimore. Greg was promoted to plant manager at Alpharma Pharmaceuticals. Rob has been obsessed with remodeling his "new" house since moving to Ridgefield a year ago. When Cara talks to Emma, she fondly refers to him as "daddy in the basement." Ryan and Elizabeth flinch every time they hear about another hurricane in the Gulf Coast region. They bought some rental properties in Pensacola Florida.

Angela, Tim, Zacchaeus, Maximilian, Kateri, Therese, and Miguel live near us in Brookfield CT. One evening I took the kids to McDonalds for dinner. Kateri, age 4, said, "Papa, there is something about you that is very strange." I said, "What?" She said, "There is a light shining out of your head." I thought, "Wow! At her age she can recognize an enlightened person! Angela's efforts at home schooling are paying rich dividends." Then I realized that what she saw was the reflection of a bright overhead light off my balding head.

As I mentioned in last year's Christmas letter, our kids have diagnosed me as autistic and Mary as having ADD (attention deficit disorder). One consequence of this is that I tend to do only one thing at a time while Mary naturally does several things concurrently. Sometimes her actions leave me speechless. Recently, upon entering the bathroom adjacent to our master bedroom, I observed her simultaneously pulling on her panty hose, brushing her teeth, and talking on the telephone. There is no doubt in my mind that I am the only person in the history of the world that has had the opportunity to observe such a unique phenomenon. I expect that when we all get to

Christmas picture 2005.

Ryan, Elizabeth,
Trinity, Christopher, Grace

Nicholas, Heidi, and Nicholas Paris

The Sherwoods: Christie, Greg,
Katie, Justin

Marianne, Heather, Russell

The Locks:
Zacchaeus, Maximilian, Tim, Angela, Miguel, Therese, Kate

Rob, Cara, Emma, James

Tim and Nichole Quinn

Bob and Mary

December 2006

Dear Friends,

Merry Christmas from the YOUNGs! Mary asked me to write a short letter with the annual highlights.

Our family continues to grow. On September 1st Philomena Mary Lock was incarnated. She was welcomed by her parents, Angela and Tim, and by her siblings, Zacchaeus, Maximilian, Kateri, Therese, and Miguel. Angela was able to squeeze in the birth between conducting her morning home-school classes and doing her afternoon activities of buying furniture and drapes. The addition of Philomena has increased the number of members in the "Young family" to thirty-one and brings the total number of grandchildren to fourteen. What a blessing!

Heather graduated from Binghamton University with her nursing degree in May. She works in the ICU at Mercy Medical Center on Long Island. She continues to improve her nursing skills on the job. One of her assigned patients is still alive. Now that she has a job, she has joined the club of credit-worthy Americans. As a result, she bought a new silver Toyota with a CD player that holds six CDs. She is temporarily subleasing a room in an apartment with three other people.

Marianne graduated with a Master's Degree in Special Education from the College of New Rochelle in New York. After a long job search and a lot of prayers, Divine Providence intervened at the last moment and she was offered a job in a public elementary school in Newtown, Connecticut, only ten miles from her apartment in Danbury. The job and environment are perfect for her and, as a result, her personality is changing from "shy little mouse" to "confident raging lion." She was explaining to Kateri Lock, age 6, that one of her students is blind. Kateri asked, "Did you try rubbing mud on his eyes?"

Russell continues to work for Bank of America in Boston. He reports directly to the Chief Financial Officer of his division and is responsible for developing and maintaining a financial model of their business. Mary and I always knew that Russell was destined to succeed.

Nichole also works for Bank of America in Boston and is a junior executive in the area of Investment Services. She and Russell share an apartment in a high-rise building three blocks from work. On weekends she returns to Albany, NY to spend time with Tim and her animals. After suffering with allergies for years, she finally took the test to determine what was causing the reactions. Turns out she is allergic to almost everything, including dust. So she invested in a vacuum cleaner and is now reading the instruction manual. Tim and Nichole were brave enough to host the "family camping outing" again this year.

Christie, Greg, Justin, and Katie are moving from Maryland to the "South" (North Carolina). Greg is the plant manager for a pharmaceutical company. One of the employees thought that Greg was not an American because of his "strange accent"! In

Maryland, Justin was voted President of his fifth grade class. After the flush of victory Christie noticed that he seemed a little dejected. He explained, "Now I'll have to deliver on the promises I made during the campaign." Children are so innocent.

Things have settled down somewhat for Rob, Cara, Emma, and James now that Robert has finished his basement remodeling project. Fortunately for the financial health of the local Home Depot store, Rob is continuing to make additional improvements in his yard.

Heidi, Nicholas, and Nicholas are doing well. To minimize the confusion with having two males in the family with the same name, Heidi and Nicholas refer to their child as "The Kid." But then he refers to his parents as "Heidi" and "Nick." Nicholas was hired by Gallo wines and is responsible for interfacing to the distributors and marketing the Gallo brand to restaurants and hotels in the greater New York area. After a break from painting during her pregnancy, Heidi is painting again between motherly tasks serving "The Kid."

Ryan and Elizabeth upgraded their environment and moved into a larger home eight miles from Poughkeepsie. Christopher, Trinity, and Grace are really enjoying the extra space and the rural atmosphere. Ryan loved the four-acre lawn . . . until he mowed it the first time. Christopher tuned into his dad's political views this election year. He told his teacher, "My dad is going to vote for the people that won't take his money."

As a gift for Mary's 60th birthday, I took her to the world's largest zoo: Africa. We went on a safari in Kenya. Christie and Greg joined us. Mary loved it! I went along as the photographer. I took over 800 pictures. As part of the safari, we went on a hot-air balloon ride. It was fabulous! We saw an incredible number of animals. Fortunately the lions that walked about 10 feet from our Land Rover thought that we were part of the environment and didn't recognize us as food. I didn't have as much faith as the others in this respect. I tried to look like spinach in case the carnivores suddenly decided that we were dinner.

It appears that I'll have to add several names to our Christmas distribution list. Mary has developed excellent relationships with all the "taster people" at Costco.

As I continue to experience the aging process, I am very aware that my waistline is migrating lower on my body. I've been able to compensate on top by ordering shirts from the Big and Tall catalog. However, I'm unable to find a corresponding catalog for pants. I've searched the internet and found no matches for the following: Big and Short, Fat and Dumpy, Plump and Petite, Stocky and Squat, Thick and Low, Wide and Truncated, Stout and Short, Stubby and Stunted, and Chubby and Compressed. Ideas anyone?

Mary and I celebrated our 40th wedding anniversary this year. Now that our youngest, Heather, is gainfully employed, we have completed this phase of our lives. We are excited about entering the "golden years" and discovering what Providence has in store for us.

We look forward to hearing from you. May God bless you and your family in 2007!

With Peace, Joy, and Love,

Bob and Mary Young, & Family

Christmas picture 2006.

Rob, James, Emma, Cara

The Locks:
Angela, Miguel, Zacchaeus, Maximilian, Philomena, Tim
Kateri, Therese

Christopher, Elizabeth, Grace, Ryan, Trinity

Tim and Nichole Quinn

Marianne, Heather, Russell

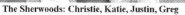

The Sherwoods: Christie, Katie, Justin, Greg

Bob and Mary

Heidi, Nicholas and Nicholas Paris

December 2007

Dear Friends,

Merry Christmas from the YOUNGs! Theresa Grace Paris, our fifteenth grandchild, was born on September 8th. She was welcomed into this world by her parents, Heidi and Nicholas, and her two-year-old brother, Nicholas. At the end of Sunday Mass recently, the priest said to the congregation, ". . . and don't forget to count your blessings!" I heard young Nicholas respond in a loud voice, "ONE . . . TWO . . . THREE . . . " Theresa's father is the only person I know who has caught a huge meddlesome beaver in a metal garbage can and transported the resisting trespasser to a lake several miles away.

Heather is sporting a beautiful engagement ring. Her fiancé, Mike Kid, created a scrapbook filled with memorable photos of their life together, summarized everything in a heartfelt poem he wrote, and popped the big question as they sat on the beach and watched the sunrise. She managed to blurt out ". . . yes, I'll marry you . . ." between her tears and sobs. The wedding is planned for next fall. Heather lives on Long Island and is a nurse in the ICU at Mercy Medical Center. She continues to gain experience both on and off the job. Recently some of her nursing cohorts felt quite accomplished when they managed to calm down an 80-year-old man who was asking for his mother. They worked very hard to convince him that she was safe and happy in the hereafter. Needless to say they had to revamp their approach when they discovered that the 102-year-old woman shuffling slowly down the hall was, in fact, his mother coming to visit. Picking roommates was another learning experience for Heather. She used the internet to find two young female roommates who sublet a room to her. At first Heather was impressed to discover that her roommates were in the "modeling" business. Later Heather complained to me that she found it disruptive when they had older male clients coming and going throughout the day and night. I became suspicious about the kind of modeling that was going on, so I intervened by sprinkling Holy Water and Blessed Salt around the apartment and under their massage table. Shortly thereafter Heather moved out of the apartment. A few weeks later her roommates decided to leave town. Apparently their modeling business went into an unexplainable slump.

Russell continues to work for Bank of America in Boston. He weathered some significant changes this year. Nichole was transferred to New York, so he had to find a new roommate and a new apartment. His boss was also transferred, so he is working for a new boss. He has adapted very well and continues to enjoy his position. For his last assignment he was asked to help decide how to spend $140 million dollars to startup a new business within the bank. Spending money is a skill that he acquired on his own while attending college. He's very, very good at that! I think the executives at the bank were impressed with how quickly he met the business challenge.

Marianne continues to teach Special Education in Newtown, CT. Despite a significant year-to-year student workload increase she seems to be surviving. Recently one of her students said, "Miss Young, Miss Young, you have a zit on your chin." Marianne responded, "Matty, you should keep those observations in your head and not say them aloud." Matty said, "Okay, Miss Young." Then, after a thoughtful pause, he continued, "But Miss Young, the zit is still there."

Tim Quinn has now joined the ranks of the Young family who has made a pilgrimage to Medjugorje. Since returning he seems to be trying hard to keep up a façade of normalcy. Nichole continues to buy and raise exotic animals, with Tim's help. They now have three alpacas.

Last summer Rob and Cara went on a vacation weekend. Mary and I babysat Emma and James. James has a very mellow personality. Emma is very verbal, and observant. During Mass she asked Cara, "What is Russell chewing?" Cara said quietly, "He's chewing gum. He shouldn't be doing that." Emma whispered, "Don't tell the priest."

Mary and I spent a couple of days babysitting for Ryan and Elizabeth when they went on a cruise. Christopher, Trinity, and two-year old Grace are very self-sufficient. Our family wonders if their skill is acquired through parental training, as Ryan claims, or through the primal instinct to survive. Ryan and Elizabeth take good care of each other. Ryan shot a skunk so that it wouldn't bother Elizabeth and the kids. Elizabeth bought Ryan a 60-inch TV, a high-powered computer to use exclusively to run his video games, and a top-of-the-line hot-tub.

Mary and I made two trips to North Carolina this year to visit Christie, Greg, Justin and Katie. They live near Charlotte. I found MapQuest helpful when I needed to find a route from their guest room to the kitchen. We attended Katie's First Communion and Grandparents Day at her school. Justin started playing football this year. Unfortunately he broke his arm so his sports career path to the NFL has been significantly impacted.

Angela and Tim are working on their time schedule. They are the only people I know that continually attempt to fit 36 hours of activities into a 24 hour day. But then time flies when you're having fun! Angela's siblings are observing closely the Lock's monastic life-style experiment to determine what to emulate and what to avoid. We send Marianne into the compound on Tuesdays and Fridays to observe and report back. Every day Zacchaeus, Maximilian, Kateri, Therese, Miguel, and Philomena attend Mass at 6:30 AM with their parents. The kids are remarkably well-behaved and learned. We're not sure if it's the Mass, the home-schooling, the absence of a TV in their home, or the genes passed down from their grandparents.

Mary and I participated in two family reunions this year. My sister, Mary Jean, and her husband, Orrin, successfully hosted the first "Young" family reunion in the Chicago area. Later Mary and I joined her siblings for a land tour and sea cruise in Alaska. The highlights for me included the landing on a glacier in a helicopter and the raft trip down a river. The most notable quote on our Alaskan jaunt was made by a young woman who moved to Alaska because the number of male residents outnumbers the females 10 to 1. After a year in Alaska, she told an inquiring female friend, "Yes, the *odds* are *good* here. But you should know that the *goods* are *odd*."

About a year ago Mary suggested we scan and digitize the family pictures so that we could give our kids a complete set for Christmas. I said innocently, "Why not?" I thought at the time that she had about 20 albums. No big deal, right? Since then we have scanned and indexed over 25,000 pictures. We had albums in places I didn't know existed. I realize now that I am living in a picture album disguised as a house, and with a photo junkie disguised as a wife and mother.

We look forward to hearing from you. May God bless you and your family in 2008!

With Peace, Joy, and Love,

Bob and Mary Young, & Family

Christmas picture 2007.

Cara, Emma, Rob, James

Tim and Nichole Quinn

The Sherwoods: Greg, Justin, Christie, Katie

The Locks:
Back Row: Miguel, Tim, Philomena, Angela
Front Row: Maximilian, Zacchaeus, Kateri, Therese

Bob and Mary

Elizabeth, Grace, Ryan, Trinity, Christopher

Marianne, Russell, Heather

Paris Family: Nicholas, Nicholas, Theresa, Heidi

December 2008

Dear Friends,

Merry Christmas from the YOUNGs! Mary asked me to write a short letter with the annual highlights.

This year will be remembered for the massive financial collapse and the resulting impact on the temporal welfare of all Americans. Fortunately for the Young family this has been a banner year with respect to our Eternal assets: our grandchildren. Our portfolio has grown 20%—from 15 to 18. What a blessing!

Our first dividend, Marguerite Mary Lock, arrived on May 19th. She was welcomed by her parents, Angela and Tim, and her 6 siblings: Zacchaeus, Maximilian, Kateri, Therese, Miguel, and Philomena. When Angela's labor pains ensued, she elected to delay the trip to the hospital in order to minimize her time in the labor room. I wasn't too involved until Mary came to me and said, "Bob, Angela thinks she may deliver the baby during the 30 mile trip to the hospital. So do you want to go with her? Or do you want to stay home and babysit her six kids?" Needless to say, my decision was made in a nanosecond. Never in my life have I had such a strong desire to babysit! As it turned out, Angela made it to the hospital ER two minutes before Marguerite was born. After Marguerite was brought home from the hospital, Marianne asked Miguel, "What will Marguerite eat?" Miguel said, "Milk." Marianne: "From where?" Miguel: "From Mom's two big bumps."

Our second dividend, Mary Rose Young, arrived on July 27th. She joined her parents, Ryan and Elizabeth, and her three siblings: Christopher, Trinity, and Grace. After the birth Mary and I were helping Elizabeth with the kids and I verbalized an off-color word. Three-year-old Grace spoke up quickly and loudly, "Grandpa is going to have to take a time-out!"

Our third Eternal dividend, Colton James Quinn, arrived on October 21st. He was welcomed by his excited parents, Nichole and Tim, and their alpaca, Cotton, formerly called Colton. According to Tim Lock, our family psychologist, the newly-named Cotton seems to be exhibiting symptoms of MPD (Multiple Personality Disorder) subsequent to Nichole borrowing his original name for her first-born.

In addition to reaping Eternal dividends this year, a significant investment was made in the Young family's grandchild production capacity. Heather and Mike Kid were married on September 20th. They are living on Long Island. Mike works for HSBC in the business loans department. Heather works as a nurse in the neurological ICU at North Shore University Hospital. I think Mike knew that Heather is frugal, like her mother. But he was not completely aware that she is also an accomplished scavenger. This became painfully evident when they moved her huge collection of random acquisitions into their one-bedroom apartment. I'm sure he was silently asking himself, "Why do we need three used bread-makers?"

Rob and Cara are planning to deliver our first Eternal dividend of 2009. Our nineteenth grandchild is scheduled to join her siblings, Emma and James, in March.

Last summer we babysat the two kids. Following his bath, Mary said to three-year-old James, "James, you smell delicious!" James said, "Yes, but don't eat me. I'm a boy. I'm not fruit!"

Heidi and Nicholas live near us, so we see their kids, Nicholas and Theresa, frequently. Recently Heidi scolded 3 year-old Nicholas when he misbehaved. He looked up, pointed to heaven, and said, "I'm sorry, God."

Marianne continues to teach Special Education in Newtown, CT. Russell works for Bank of America in Boston. He received a major promotion in February. Marianne and Russell both tried the on-line dating approach to search for a future mate. Marianne used CatholicMatch.com and was very successful in finding someone with similar values. Russell's criteria continue to evolve. He used a different service (HotBod.com I think?) and was less successful. He now realizes that when a girl checks the "slender" box to describe her body type, she is apparently using that word in its broadest sense.

Again this year the Quinn's hosted the extended Young family at a campout—all 34 of us. The Sherwood's (Christie, Greg, Justin, and Katie) flew up from North Carolina. Greg had just completed a "half" Iron-Man triathlon, which is a 70 mile race consisting of three parts: swimming, cycling, and running. I asked Greg, "Which is harder: racing in the triathlon, or spending a weekend camping with the Young's?" He flashed a smile mixed with pain and quipped, "That's an easy question to answer!"

Based on our family's expertise with camping and community, a decision was made to *franchise* our experience. Prompted by the Holy Spirit, Ryan led an effort to organize Camp Veritas, an outdoor, one-week camp designed to inspire and form young Catholics. Many family members helped by giving time and/or money. Fifty kids attended and were supported by thirty adult volunteers including four Franciscan Friars. Based on the camper's positive feedback this inaugural year, we expect a dramatic increase in enrollments for next August and will need significantly more adult help. Please visit our website at www.campveritas.com if you want to contribute in some way.

On December 30th of last year, I asked Mary if she had accomplished all her annual goals. She said, "Yes, all but one." I said, "What's that?" She said, "Lose 20 pounds." After a pause she continued with a resolute tone in her voice, "But I still have over 24 hours to go."

I turned 65 in September, and have joined the ranks of those people on Medicare. Since retiring five years ago, I have enjoyed my solitude, and have become somewhat reclusive. Most of my interaction with the outside world is with my kids. In preparation for Heather's wedding, however, it was necessary for me to have a phone conversation with a young man from Marriott Hotels. Following a long, intense, animated exchange with him, I said, "Thank you for your help." Then I continued with my habitual closing, "Bye . . . I love you."

Well, the longest election in U.S. history has finally concluded. While Barak Obama's stance on abortion was a deal-breaker for pro-life people like me, I hope he can run the country as effectively as he ran his campaign for president. Meanwhile, based on the evolving attitudes of the electorate, it looks like the battle between the "culture of life" and the "culture of death" will intensify as our planetary spaceship careens towards the inevitable Final Judgment.

We look forward to hearing from you. May God bless you and your family in 2009!

With Peace, Joy, and Love,

Bob and Mary Young

Christmas picture 2008. Note that Nichole is pregnant with Colton.

December 2009

Dear Friends,

Merry Christmas from the YOUNGs! Mary asked me to write a short letter with the annual highlights.

Our family continues to expand. We have added two grandchildren, bringing our total to 20.

Averie Grace Young arrived on March 11th. She was welcomed by her parents, Rob and Cara, and her two siblings, Emma and James. While we were babysitting the kids recently, Emma said to Mary, "Grandma, why is your hair white?" Mary responded, "Because that's the way God made it." Emma smiled and quipped, "That's okay. I'll love you anyway."

Justice Michael Young was born on November 17th. He joined his parents, Ryan and Elizabeth, and his four siblings: Christopher, Trinity, Grace, and Mary Rose. A few weeks ago Grandma Mary was feeding lunch to Grace (4) and Mary Rose (1). Grandma said, "Did you kids pray your grace before eating?" Grace replied, "Mary is too young to pray." Grandma looked at Mary Rose and asserted, "Mary, you can pray, can't you?" Again, an exasperated Grace intervened. "Grandma, she can't even say 'No' yet."

Now that Mary and I are "retired", we are available to drive travelers to the airport. In October, Doctor Tim Lock departed for a two week working trip to Australia, leaving behind Angela and his seven kids: Zacchaeus, Maximilian, Kateri, Therese, Miguel, Philomena, and Marguerite. Despite Tim making a five page list of what to bring, we had to backtrack to pick up something important that he forgot to put on his list: "SUITCASE". Earlier this year, Angela awoke at 3:35 AM and found Kateri fully clothed for Mass with her hair brushed and reading a book. Angela asked, "Do you know what time it is?" Kateri, "I got up at 5:25." Angela, "I think you misread the digital clock. It was 2:25, not 5:25. Please go back to bed."

Marianne spends a lot of time at the Lock's helping Angela with the kids and scavenging food. She gave Miguel (4) a tour of her apartment. When he went home later that day, he reported to Angela, "Marianne is really poor. She has no food in her refrigerator and she has to put pennies in the washing machine to pay to get her clothes cleaned."

Mary and I were very involved in supporting Heidi and Nick in their process of building a new house and selling their existing home. They moved in July. We gave them a long list of "hints and tips" that we accumulated through our experiences over the years. Thanks to our input, Nick has a bigger garage and Heidi has a double oven. Last December Heidi said to Nicholas (4), "Christmas is coming." He asked, "Well, where is it?" In November Heidi finally decided to potty-train Theresa (2). The impetus for this came when Theresa came to Heidi with a pained expression on her face and urgently insisted, "I want to go poopy in the potty!"

Mary and I also helped Heather and Mike fix up their first home they bought in November. I took the leadership role on painting and electrical. Meanwhile, Mary worked with Mike and they replaced the baseboard heater metal covers. Heather specialized in cleaning and painting. The transformation of the older home was quite remarkable and very exhilarating.

Russell continues to search for the woman of his dreams, although the profile of this perfect woman seems to be evolving. His requirements went from "hot and rich" to "holy" to "holy with child-bearing hips". Earlier this year both Russell and Nichole joined the ranks of the unemployed. The entire investment group within Bank of America was eliminated in the financial tsunami that followed the decision by the Bank of America CEO to purchase the failing Merrill Lynch. After an extended, unplanned vacation, Russell found work with Citizens Bank which is located south of Boston. To celebrate, he bought himself a new car—his first! Meanwhile, Nichole is enjoying her semi-retirement status and spending full time with one-year-old Colton. She and Tim made a major renovation to their house to accommodate their first child, nearly doubling the size. This year they again hosted the annual extended family outing and, with the larger, modernized home, the 37 of us "camped" in relative comfort.

I mentioned Camp Veritas in last year's Christmas letter. This is the outdoor, one-week camp designed to inspire and form young Catholics. This year we more than doubled our enrollments over 2008. We had 120 kids attend supported by 40 adult volunteers, including my brother, John, and my sister, Mary Jean. Christie also flew up from North Carolina to help, and brought along Justin, my first grandchild to attend as a camper. Katie stayed with Nichole and attended the closing ceremony. Heather, Mike, Rob, Marianne, and Russell joined Ryan, Elizabeth, Mary and me in leading this family ministry. Tim Quinn and Nick Paris helped as chaperones last year, but were unavailable this year. We are excited, and apprehensive, that the enrollment may double again in 2010. We will definitely need more chaperones! Please visit our website at www.campveritas.com to check out the camp.

Mary worries that my addiction to Haagen Dazs ice cream is unhealthy. Luckily for me, Haagen Dazs saved my life! Turns out I had a burst appendix in April and, according to my doctor, the reason I didn't get a serious infection is that the fat in my abdomen caused a protective wall to be formed isolating the deadly germs. Praise God for Haagen Dazs!

Meanwhile, the frequency of "senior moments" is increasing for Mary and me. In October, Mary and I were painting the inside of Heidi's new garage. Mary came over and whispered, "Bob, have you seen my cell phone? I can't find it." I responded calmly. "Yes. I know where it is. You are holding it to your left ear and are using it to have a conversation with Christie."

We look forward to hearing from you. May God bless you and your family in 2010!

With Peace, Joy, and Love,

Bob and Mary Young

Christmas picture 2009. Note that Elizabeth is pregnant with Justice.

December 2010

Dear Friends,

Merry Christmas from the YOUNGs! Mary asked me to write a short letter with the annual highlights.

Our family continues to expand. We have added two grandchildren, bringing our total to 22.

Felicity Mary Lock arrived on May 17th. She was welcomed by her parents, Tim and Angela, and her seven siblings: Zacchaeus, Maximilian, Kateri, Therese, Miguel, Philomena, and Marguerite. After Felicity was born, Marianne decided to move in with the Locks to be of some help. Angela and Tim do a great job teaching their kids about Christianity. Tim used a large nail to explain to them in graphic detail how Jesus was nailed to the cross. Miguel (age 5), eyes wide in fearful disbelief, insisted, "*I don't* want to be a martyr!"

Luke Alexander Paris was born on June 5th. He joined his parents, Heidi and Nicholas, and his two siblings: Nicholas and Theresa. Last Christmas, Nicholas (age 4) noticed Heidi putting up Christmas stockings. He asserted, "Santa is going to bring us presents!" Heidi said, "No, not exactly." Then Heidi went into a lengthy and rambling explanation concluding with the following statement: ". . . so the concept of Santa comes from Saint Nicholas, who is a saint in Heaven." A few days later, when a friend of Heidi's came to the house, young Nicholas sadly explained, "Santa is dead." However, the next day during a trip to the mall, he saw Santa talking to several young kids. He shouted, "Santa is alive! He has been born again!" I'm sure that Nicholas will be fine after a few weeks of psychotherapy.

Heather and Mike are enjoying their "new" house on Long Island. They have spent a year making improvements to their first home. They have a very nice neighbor who is traditional in his beliefs regarding male and female roles. Heather was working in the yard when he came by the first time to introduce himself. When he asked about Mike, Heather explained, "He's in the kitchen making dinner." A few days later, the neighbor approached Mike, who was working in the yard, and struck up a conversation. He seemed relieved to see Mike doing the "man's work". As the conversation evolved, he casually asked, "Is Heather around?" Mike said, "Yes. She's up on the roof repairing the chimney."

Christie and Greg have decided to continue living in North Carolina, after recently considering a work-related move to the North. They enjoy the warmer climate and the more relaxed southern way of life. Justin and Katie are actively involved in school and sports. Greg is a glutton for punishment and participates in 70 mile triathlons regularly. Christie participates in the triathlons also . . . she watches Greg. Mary and I spent time with the Sherwood's this fall. Christie has her family room decorated with candy . . . not *fake* candy, but *real* candy. And, as part of her exhibit, she has several variants of Reese's

Peanut Butter cups displayed (some are cups, some are eggs, etc.). It was emotionally overwhelming for me to spend time in that room, given my addictions. The peanut butter eggs, particularly, each with its soft, smooth chocolate shell holding snugly inside the delectable bite-sized morsel of heaven, were not safe from me. I sent an e-mail warning to the rest of the family.

Russell is now working in Connecticut for Jefferies, a Financial Investment company. It's great to have him close to home again. He enjoys his new job. He feels that his work associates are pretty weird people. He relates to them extremely well.

Rob, Cara, and their three kids (Emma, James, and Averie) are enjoying their home. Now that Rob has finished most of his inside improvements, he is focusing on his yard. Like his mother, however, he enjoys getting a good deal. When he found out he could get wood chips at no cost, he signed up. Before long his yard looked like a scene out of a movie called "*Bucky Beaver and His Friends Pig Out!*" James recently asked, "What does the word 'Nun' mean?" Then answering himself, said, "I know. Nun means they have nothing, they have 'Nun'."

Nichole and Tim are enjoying immensely their son, Colton, who turned *two* last month. They taught him "baby sign language" shortly after he was born, and it's quite remarkable. The three of them can carry on a conversation without uttering a spoken word. They have also signed up to be foster parents for kids that need a temporary home. They currently have a young girl with Cystic Fibrosis staying with them. They seem to be adapting to parenthood quite effectively. Last month Nichole and Colton were visiting Christie and her family in North Carolina. Colton dumped some milk on the floor, so Nichole gave him a paper towel to wipe it up. Justin, Christie's oldest, watched in amazement as 2-year-old Colton obediently and routinely cleaned the floor under the watchful eye of his mother.

Under the leadership of Ryan, the Camp Veritas family ministry continues to flourish. He is supported by Elizabeth, his five kids (Christopher, Trinity, Grace, Mary, and Justice), and several other family members including Mary and me. During this third year of the week-long camp we hosted 185 teenagers and 70 adult volunteers. Archbishop Timothy Dolan celebrated the closing Mass. Every participant was given a copy of Ryan's new book called "*Climbing Veritas Mountain: One Man's Journey with the Lord*" which highlights some of the key truths taught at camp. If you want to volunteer, go to www.campveritas.com for more information.

At 2:15 AM on Friday, November 5th, I awoke from a deep sleep and became immediately aware of an intruder in our bedroom. Mary woke up also and watched in terror as I engaged in a fight to the death with our unwelcome guest. Armed only with a toilet plunger and my nerves of steel, I managed to snuff out the life of the nocturnal attacker. As I flushed the furry creature down the toilet, Mary emotionally exclaimed, "Oh, Bob, you are my hero!" As I gazed at her face, which was flushed with admiration,

I replied humbly, "Aw, shucks. It twasn't nuthin." Later I wondered if I should have kept the carcass of the mouse and had the head mounted, like Tim Quinn did with the 10 point buck he shot. Oh, well . . . maybe next time.

With Peace, Joy, and Love,

Bob and Mary Young

Christmas 2010.

December 2011

Dear Friends,

Merry Christmas from the YOUNGs! Mary asked me to write a short letter with the annual highlights.

Our family continues to expand. We have added one grandchild, bringing our total to 23. Colby Maximilian Kid arrived on November 6th. He was welcomed by his parents, Heather and Mike. Mary and I were somewhat delighted when they named him Colby. A couple of months prior to his birth they told us they were going to name him Elmo, after St. Erasmus who was fondly called St. Elmo. We prefer the name Colby to either Erasmus or Elmo.

Christie and Greg are still in North Carolina. They bought two jet-ski's so have a new family activity for Justin and Katie. Justin is my oldest grandchild and will get his driver's license next May when he turns 16. Greg already has some gray hair, so a few extra gray hairs would be nearly imperceptible. I don't know for sure, but I suspect Christie's hair color may continue to stay dark brown with a little help from her hairdresser.

This summer Tim Lock and Zacchaeus, Maximilian, Kateri, and Therese traveled to Spain to attend the World Youth Day hosted by Pope Benedict XVI. The kids belong to a choir that sings in Latin and had the opportunity to sing at a number of venues in Spain. Angela remained home and took care of the four youngest kids: Miguel, Philomena, Marguerite, and Felicity. Prior to the Spain trip, Mary was driving all eight kids home after choir practice in the Lock maxi-van when some threatening weather suddenly developed. There was a tornado warning. In an attempt to calm the younger siblings, Zacchaeus said, "Don't worry. Tornadoes only take beautiful people, not ugly people." Later, after the group arrived home at the Lock's, Miguel, age 6, in the presence of his mother, Angela, stared intently at Mary's face and said, "Grandma, you have lots of scratches (wrinkles) on your face. I am very glad you're ugly." Mary had to intervene quickly to protect Miguel from a shocked Angela and explain the context of his loving comment.

Marianne also traveled to Spain and spent a full month there. In addition to the World Youth Day event, she visited friends and did some sightseeing. The highlight of her trip, however, was an intense spiritual Ignatian retreat. She continues to serve humanity via her job as a special education teacher in Newtown, Connecticut; her volunteer CCD role; and her service to the Lock family.

Nichole, Tim, and Colton hosted the immediate family again for the annual family outing. The intimate gathering of the 40 of us had a great time. Tim built an outdoor shower for us; it was quite ingenious. While I'm sure Tim's project was motivated primarily out of love, there was also a practical aspect. He has a fragile septic system and too much water could create a serious problem. As they say, "Waste happens!" Also, it's very convenient to have medical professionals in the family. Ryan looked at Tim during the family gathering and said, "You have cancer on your skin." Tim had his growth biopsied to confirm the diagnosis, and then had it cut out.

Russell decided to abandon the high-pressure Wall Street lifestyle in the Banking and Securities Industry. He moved to Albany, New York, and is working as a senior financial analyst in a manufacturing company. While he anticipates that the bonuses may be smaller, so is the stress. He loves leaving work at noon and going home two blocks away for a relaxing lunch.

In January, Rob, Cara, Emma, James, and Avery were sledding. Rob wiped out and broke his cheekbone in 3 places. He was pretty happy to get three weeks off work. Later in the year, Rob said to James, "You are one good looking kid. You must have inherited your good looks from your dad." Without hesitation James responded, "No. I got my good looks from God."

Ryan and Elizabeth enjoy an extremely active life. They have full-time jobs, lead the rapidly expanding Camp Veritas project, and nurture their five creations: Christopher, Trinity, Grace, Mary Rose, and Justice. In October, with Christopher and Trinity joining them, they were able to cruise the Mediterranean and take side trips to a number of places including Rome and the Vatican.

In November, Heidi and Nicholas spent a week in Spain lounging in a mountain villa. Nicholas speaks to his kids in Spanish to teach them the language. So Nicholas and Theresa went with them and were able to practice their speaking skills with the natives. Much to Heidi's relief, Mary and I were available to take care of 18-month-old Luke. The first words Luke spoke at age one were "Hola, Dad." One night Theresa, age three, called out to Heidi from her room, "Mommy, the pee fell out of my body!"

Mary and I celebrated our 45th wedding anniversary this year. We renewed our vows at Mass and the kids hosted a family party afterwards. As we get older, it is getting more difficult for Mary and me to "recall" words. That's particularly true for the names of our grandchildren. I sometimes wonder if there is a conspiracy to confuse us. We now have grandkids with the following names: Colby and Colton; Justice and Justin; Therese and Theresa; Katie and Kateri. I thought we were safe from confusion with the names Zacchaeus and Miguel; but the conspiracy will be confirmed if future grandkids are named Amadeus and Manuel. I've thought of using social security numbers for unique identification, but that may be a problem with the U.S. government. So now I'm thinking of using e-mail ID's. Suggestions are welcomed!

I started writing my annual Christmas letters in 1975. That was 36 years ago. This will be the first year that I'm going to expand my letter beyond two pages. Why? Because when I wrote an e-mail to my kids and asked for some anecdotes for my Christmas letter, Heidi responded with a page full of observations made by Nicholas, age 5. When others saw his observations, they insisted that I include ALL of them in my Christmas letter. Thus, you will find them below. Enjoy!

With Peace, Joy, and Love,

Bob and Mary Young

Observations made by Nicholas Paris, age 5, and Theresa Paris, age 3 follow (the "I" is Heidi):

- Nicholas said, "Mom, Heaven is going to be a tough place." When I asked him "why", he responded, "Well God kicked one angel out!"

- Nicholas was praying out loud in front of the Mary statue at church. He poured out his heart to her. He said, "Mary, thank you for Jesus. Please help the poor people and the people in Purgatory . . . Oh, and I like your dress."

- I was making eggs while holding baby Luke. I accidentally left a shell in Nicholas' egg and he declared, "Mom, I just bit down on something hard and I think it was the chicken's foot!"

- Nicholas was a sensation at his pre-school summer class. When all the moms were picking up their children, the kids were in a circle around Nicholas who was showing off his impressive Spanish skills. One boy told his mom, "He sounds just like Dora! (a Spanish-speaking TV character)"

- Nicholas played the board game "Sorry" in the morning before everyone woke up. He would switch sides to pretend he was moving his opponent's players and then switch again to do his own. When I woke up he happily announced, "Mom, I keep on winning!"

- When I started letting Nicholas dress himself sometimes he accidentally left on two pairs of underwear and we would not notice until the day was over. We laughed about it so one night he played a trick on me. He was giggling as I discovered he was wearing 7 pairs of socks!

- Nicholas and Theresa were playing "Heaven". They were sitting with soft blankets around them and Nicholas explained the blankets are the very special car seats that they need to get to Heaven.

- Nicholas said, "Mom, can I eat a grasshopper one day to show God how much I love Him just like John the Baptist did?"

- When I asked Nicholas why there were pee drips in the middle of the bathroom floor he responded, "Well, I closed my eyes while I was praying to God. I couldn't see where I was peeing so I got it everywhere."

- Nicholas said, "Mom, Theresa is making Jesus frustrated because she took all my Legos."

- When my friend Grace was sleeping in the library room on the floor, I heard Nicholas and Theresa debating as they watched her through the glass door. Nicholas said, "I think she is like a leprechaun and does not really sleep." Theresa responded, "No, I think she sleeps like the rest of us."

- One day at lunch Nicholas and Theresa were having an in-depth conversation. Nicholas was explaining the difference between statues and human beings. He said, "Statues don't move. They are sometimes white or brown. They are different from human beings. Nobody ever tells you what human beings are . . . you have to figure it out by yourself. People will just keep saying the words "human beings" to you and you never know what it means . . . you have to figure it out all by yourself. I will try to explain it to you so you know what people are talking about when they say "human beings" . . . ."

- One time when baby Luke laughed, Nicholas happily yelled, "Mom, Luke laughed like a real human!"

- Theresa and Nicholas were told to pick up their toys in the basement. When they asked for my help, I said, "No" because I was cleaning other parts of the house. They responded by saying, "Mom, what would Jesus do in this situation?"

- We were talking about how one day Nicholas and Theresa would be old enough to choose a confirmation name and add it to their names. It was explained to them that they could choose the name of their favorite Saint. Nicholas responded, "I know what my confirmation name will be. It will be Nicholas GOD Paris."

- Nicholas: "If I get a cut in my belly button all my air will come out and I will die. I will be like a bear without his stuffing!"

- Nicholas was showing me his paper checker-board that he was making for God and the Saints. He explained that when he died he was going to play checkers with them on this checkerboard in heaven!

- Nicholas: "Which one of my feet is older?"

- Nicholas: "I want more of that Chicken Farmer John (Chicken Parmesan)."

- Nicholas came to me one night after he had been in bed 20 minutes already. He said, "Mom, I made a drip of pee in my pants." I asked him, "Why" and he said, "Well I really needed to come and tell you about my cough. I knew that wasn't enough of an 'emergency' to get out of my bed without getting into trouble. I know that when I wet my bed it *is* considered an emergency, Mom, and then you don't get me into trouble. I asked God if I should wet just a little so I could get out of my bed to tell you about my cough. He said, "Yes" so I did."

- Nicholas met the nun at grandma's and grandpa's house and told us, "Mom and Dad, when I grow up I want to be a nun so I can pray all the time."

- Nicholas: "Last night I had a real emergency on my nose. It was called blood."

- Theresa and Nicholas one day were spitting their milk into a second cup. They said, "This is the spit cup just like Daddy uses for his wine tests!"

- Theresa ran to the potty after making a drip in her underwear. I said, "Theresa, What happened?" She replied, "Mom, I forgive you" (she is still learning the difference between "I'm sorry" and "I forgive you").

- Theresa was in her room during naps and she was calling out for someone to bring her favorite bear. Nicholas was trying to squeeze the bear under the crack in her door. I saved the situation by rescuing the poor bear. Theresa exclaimed in the end, "Wow, that bear's life was saved! He was almost squished into Heaven!"

- We were talking about our favorite Saints like Saint Nicholas and Saint Theresa, and Theresa said, "My favorite Saint is Saint Mommy!"

- Theresa exclaimed while we were driving, "There goes a Mickey Bus!" It took me a minute to realize that she meant *mini-bus* (and Minnie is Mickey's friend so it confused Theresa!).

- I told Theresa that Mom and Dad are the bosses of the house and the kids need to listen to us. She said, "Actually Mom, God and Jesus are the bosses of this house!"

- At dinner one evening Nicholas told his family that he needed to complete the first homework assignment of his life and wanted to do it well and remember to turn it in to his teacher the next day. He said, "I really need God and Mary's help on this one. Could we pray the Rosary?" The family joined him and prayed one decade of the Rosary. At the end, Nicholas concluded by saying, "Our Lady of Perpetual Help, pray for us!"

Some older comments and/or observations:

- September 2009: Nicholas starts pre-school (age almost 4). The principal, who is a nun, said, "Nicholas, how is your day?" He responded, "Great! My penis was very itchy, but my mom gave me a bath. So it is much better now."

- January 2010: Mary said, "Nicholas, why do you have your pants on backwards?" He responded, "Because when I walk backwards, they are facing the right direction."

- June 2010: Nicholas asked, "Grandpa, why do you have a gold tooth?" Bob responded, "Because I ate too much candy." Nicholas was heard to say resolutely as he walked away, "I'm going to eat too much candy so I can get a gold tooth."

- June 2010: Bob asked, "Nicholas, why is Theresa crying? Did you hurt her?" He responded, "Not yet."

Christmas 2011. Note that Heather is pregnant with Colby.

This is a picture of Bob and Mary taken in September of 2011.

December 2012

Dear Friends,

Merry Christmas from the YOUNGs! Mary asked me to write a short letter with the annual highlights.

Two more grandchildren have arrived, bringing our total to 25. Matthew Augustine Paris left the womb on April 17th. He was welcomed by his parents, Nicholas and Heidi, and his three siblings, Nicholas (7), Theresa (5), and Luke (2). Dakota Catherine Quinn was born five days later, on April 22nd. She was welcomed by her adoptive parents Tim and Nichole, her brother, Colton (4), and members of her birth family who live in the area.

Heidi quietly walked into the family room one day and noticed that Nicholas and Theresa were standing near the TV but looking towards baby Matthew, who was lying on the floor. Nicholas asked his little sister, "Should we watch a video on TV? Or should we watch Matthew?" Theresa responded, "Let's watch Matthew," as she dragged a chair towards the recently created, real-life, action figure!

About a month before Dakota Catherine was born, Colton reminded Nichole, "We have to get the bedroom ready for 'North Dakota'." Nichole corrected him, "It's not 'North Dakota'; just 'Dakota'." Later Colton told grandma, "We have to get the bedroom ready for 'Just Dakota'."

Mary and I were blessed to have the opportunity to spend a week with Colby Kid in October. Due to the effects of Hurricane Sandy, Heather and Mike needed to use our home as their base of operations for the 10 days they were out of power. Thankfully, the huge tree in their front yard was blown over *away* from their house by the high winds. When it toppled it nearly hit their neighbors' house across the street. Colby turned one-year-old while he was here, and he went trick-or-treating his first time. Colby seems VERY HAPPY with the parents God gave him.

Tim Lock and his four oldest, Zacchaeus (16), Maximilian (14), Kateri (12), and Therese (10), were in Rome when the Hurricane hit. The Pope was canonizing Saint Kateri Tekawitha, the first native North American saint. Their two week pilgrimage was extended by five days as a result of their flight cancellation. They were grateful for the extra days in Rome . . . paid for by their trip insurance! Meanwhile, Angela was relaxing at home with the four youngest: Miguel (8), Philomena (6), Marguerite (4), and Felicity (2). She was only without power a couple of days, but had a gas-powered generator. Prior to attending Mass one morning during the time his siblings were in Rome, Miguel asked Angela, "Are there states in Italy?" Angela responded, "I don't know. But you should ask the priest because he can answer most questions like that." Marguerite was apparently listening to this conversation. So, after Mass, she walked up to the priest and asked, "Father, how are baby horses born?"

After several months of serious prayer, Marianne felt God calling her to help, in a special way, some kids in need. Her first step was to spend the month of March in Peru serving as a volunteer in an orphanage. The second leg of her journey was to begin working full time for the Locks as a teacher for their home-schooled kids. I'm not sure who is happier with the new arrangement: Angela with the newly found help? Or Marianne, who thinks she found a Heavenly niche on earth?

Cara's dad, Richard, contracted with Disneyworld to host Rob's family this year. Emma (8), James (7), and Averie (3) were pleasantly shocked to discover that a vacation to visit "Papa McEvoy" in Florida included several days of rides, events, and delicious treats! I heard a rumor that Richard will spend the next several months recovering from the "vacation". Rob was recently combing James' hair when he playfully said, "James. You are a good looking boy. You must have gotten your good looks from your father." James quickly responded. "No. I got them from God!"

Ryan and Elizabeth had another uneventful, relaxing year . . . NOT! Since they both have full time Physician Assistant jobs, it is no small task to raise their small army of Young's: Christopher (12), Trinity (10), Grace (7), Mary (4), and Justice (3). They hosted the extended Young family camping weekend this year at their home. I asked Ryan if their septic system was up to the task. He assured me, "Dad, that won't be a problem." Well, he has always been an optimist. Needless to say, in addition to our typical family activities of horse-balls, basketball, and team Frisbee, we had a contingent of adults frantically playing a new game called "Roto-Rooter: let's unclog the septic pipes." Meanwhile there were 43 family members who, for an interminably long 24 hours, used the woods behind Ryan's house as "nature's outhouse."

A month later, Ryan and Elizabeth led the effort to conduct Camp Veritas and host over 400 teen campers and 150 adult chaperones. They had to expand the camp to two separate weeks this year to handle the increased volume. During the second week Cardinal Dolan was a guest for a few hours. He engaged with the joyful campers and celebrated Holy Mass. As the Cardinal observed Christopher being himself (that is, highly animated), he jokingly said to Ryan, "You should put that kid on Ritalin!"

Despite living the farthest away from the family, Christie, Greg, Justin (16), and Katie (13) are able to frequently connect with the rest of us. This year Christie hosted Heather, Mike, Colby, and Nichole. Christie came up for the "Sibling's reunion" hosted by Heather. She also came up and brought Katie to Camp Veritas. The entire family came up for the "Roto-Rooter: let's unclog the septic pipes" game at Ryan's. When Katie came to our house, she asked me, "What is the difference between 2% milk and 1% milk?" I pinched the large roll of fat on my midsection and said, "This is 2% milk." She chuckled, pinched herself in her fat-free midsection, and said, "I guess this must be 1% milk!" Justin got his driver's license this year, the first grandchild to reach this level of responsibility. My mind is flooded with scary memories of living in Mount Kisco with a houseful of teenagers "driving" five junker cars. Memories of those years make me relieved that I'm closer to the end of my life and too old to experience THAT again. Praise God!

This year Russell met Anne, his new "life coach". He realized he needed help after he went to the doctor for his first physical checkup in many years. The doctor took his blood pressure and panicked. It took a while before the on-site response team realized that he was NOT having a heart attack. Anyway, his good friend, Anne, is now working with him to establish a healthier lifestyle. In fact, Anne suggested that he needs help 24 hours a day . . . so Russell proposed! The mutual care-giver contract will be signed in August of next year.

This year Mary and I had the opportunity to make a two week pilgrimage to several Blessed Virgin Mary apparition sites. We traveled with a group to Lourdes in France, to Fatima in Portugal, and to Garabandal in Spain. These are locations where she appeared in 1858, 1917, and 1961 respectively. Some years ago we visited Mexico where she appeared in 1531 as Our Lady of Guadalupe and had a major impact on spreading the Catholic faith to the Mexican natives. Nine years ago we traveled to Medjugorje, a village in what used to be Yugoslavia, where our Spiritual Mother appeared for the first time in 1981 as Our Lady Queen of Peace, and is still appearing daily to two of the six visionaries. The bottom line: Mary and I are very grateful that we have a Spiritual Mother who is intimately concerned with us and how we live our lives on a daily basis. We believe that her contemporary guidance via her messages is *invaluable* as we negotiate our path towards Eternity!

I got really exasperated the other day. I was trying to find out from Mary about an event that we were planning to attend that evening. In the midst of the short conversation, she started to dial her phone. I interrupted her and said, "What are you *doing*? We are *talking*. You are like a *teenager*!" Then I asked her again about the event, and she said impatiently, "I don't know any more than you do!" I said angrily, "Yes you do! *You* know what *you don't know*, and right now *I don't know* what *you don't know*!" . . . So, for you younger, married couples, this is what it means to *grow old together and have in-depth communications (if you know what I mean)*!

Due to the size of our family now (43 people), we didn't succeed in getting a photo of everyone together this year, so I made a composite. We are getting large enough now that by the next presidential election they will start to woo us as a "voting bloc".

Heidi passed on some comments made by Nicholas, age 7, and Theresa, age 5, that I thought you might find enjoyable. They follow the body of this letter. Enjoy!

With Peace, Joy, and Love,

Bob and Mary Young

Observations made by Nicholas Paris, age 7, and Theresa Paris, age 5 follow (the "I" is Heidi):

- Nicholas asked me, "Mom, where is hell? Is it in France?"

- Nicholas said, "I know there are different levels of Heaven. The lowest is near God's toenails."

- Nicholas was trying to get his newborn baby brother, Matthew, to stop crying. When he was successful, I asked him how he did it. He responded, "First, I rub Matthew's belly until he throws up. Then I speak to him like this and he smiles!"

- After I made young Nicholas a great breakfast, he came and hugged me and said, "Mom, you are the wife I always wanted."

- There was a wrapped-up surprise on the art table and Nicholas explained, "This is going to be for God for when I am in Heaven. On His birthday, He gets to open it."

- Nicholas said, "Mom, can I have more of that cereal germ thing?" (referring to wheat germ)

- Nicholas noticed that Daddy and Luke's olive colored Italian skin looked different from his own. He phrased it like this, "Daddy and Luke's skin is brown and the rest of the family has peach colored skin. Martin Luther King helped brown people so they could sit in the back of the bus!"

- Nicholas asked me to check the weather to see if we could get our Christmas tree the next day. I told him I would check the computer to see the weather forecast. He responded, "Or you could just ask God!"

- One night Nicholas got sick after eating Chinese noodles with peanut sauce. Later I heard him repeating over and over, "I never want to eat peanut butter from China again!"

- Grandma told young Nicholas that the power went out for several days in the Northeast right before his parents' wedding celebration. He loves flashlights, so he responded, "I hope the power goes out for my wedding day too!"

- Looking out the window during a rainstorm, Nicholas shouted, "It's a *tarantula* downpour!" (*torrential*)

- Theresa told her teacher, "The caterpillar is building his *raccoon*!" (*cocoon*)

- When Theresa was asked about future career choices at school, she attempted to combine Daddy's career with Gallo with her affection for Mommy. She responded, "When I grow up, I want to be a Mommy that drinks wine!"

- Later, Theresa developed alternative careers. She told everyone, "I want to be a nun . . . or if that doesn't happen, I will be a bus driver."

- Theresa loves her perfect, newborn brother and determined what his future career could be. She said, "I know what baby Matthew can be when he grows up. He can be Jesus!"

- Theresa prayed on Saint Patrick's Day, "Saint Patrick, we love you. Thank you for teaching us about the Trinity using three leaves. We know it is NOT poison ivy!"

- Looking at the star (i.e. behavior) chart, Theresa pointed to the last blank page and said, "Is this the last day we ever need to be good?

Christmas 2012.

The Sherwoods: Greg, Christie, Justin, & Katie

Marianne

Russell

2012

The Paris Family: Nicholas, Heidi, Nicholas, Theresa, Luke, & Matthew

Bob and Mary Young

The Youngs: Rob, Cara, Emma, James, & Averie

The Youngs: Ryan, Elizabeth, Christopher, Trinity, Grace, Mary, & Justice

The Quinns: Tim, Nichole, Colton, & Dakota

The Locks: Tim, Angela, Zacchaeus, Maximilian, Kateri Therese, Miguel, Philomena, Marguerite, & Felicity

The Kids: Mike, Heather, & Colby

Conclusion:

In conclusion, I remind you what I was taught by Mary, my lovely, holy wife: **The Power of a Good Woman is Unlimited!**

The words from the Book of Wisdom, Chapter 7, versus 26-27, relate to her I believe, for she is indeed a wise woman!

- . . . For she is the refulgence of eternal light, the spotless mirror of the power of God, the image of his goodness.
- . . . And she, who is one, can do all things, and renews everything while herself perduring; And *passing into holy souls from age to age*, she produces friends of God and prophets.

What now? Why did God have *you* read this book? There are **no accidents** in Life! There is only Divine Providence. Please join me and my family as we journey in Unity towards our Eternal Home and the Divine Wedding Feast!

Our home is glowing with the light of the Holy Spirit and is inviting everyone to come to the banquet of the Lord!

The banquet table is set! Come and be nourished with the life-giving food of Divine fellowship!

Recommendations:

- Visit www.calltobefree.com and browse our electronic home.

- Consider buying this book for a friend. It makes a great Christmas gift.

- Consider reading books by the author and by other family members, particularly the following:

  o *Calling All POWs* by Robert A. Young

  o *Climbing Further Up Veritas Mountain* by Ryan Paul Young

- Thank God for all the Gifts He has given you, and remember that *everything* He gives you in life is a gift, even though it may cause pain! It is *impossible* for a loving God to providentially give you something that is *not* good for your eternal soul.

- Reconcile! Reconcile with family and friends. Forgive your enemies. Reconcile with God.

About the Authors:

Bob and Mary Young have experienced 47 years of married life. They have nine children and twenty-five grandchildren. They believe that this earthly life is an adventure *in* God and *with* God, and, that by doing His Will in this odyssey, they will join Him and their loved ones in an eternal adventure of divine love in the next life!